A LONELY Rose

Poetry

By

JORDAN WELLS

Other works by Jordan Wells

LOGGED OFF: MY JOURNEY OF ESCAPING
THE SOCIAL MEDIA WORLD

MIRRORS AND REFLECTIONS

THE HEALING

THE RING PACK

IT'S FUN BEING A HUMAN BEING

MADAM PRESIDENT

Centenary Uni. Alum (Class of 11')

My
4th
Book

Signature

With Peace and Love! xoxo

Jordan
Wells

Mon.
5:18 pm

5/23/22

A LONELY *Rose*

JORDAN WELLS

Scott and Scholars Press
East Orange, New Jersey 07017

Scott and Scholars Press® is a registered trademark of
Jordan Wells Publishing.

Publisher's Cataloging-in-Publication data

Names: Wells, Jordan, author.
Title: A lonely rose / Jordan Wells.
Description: East Orange, NJ: Scott and Scholars Press, 2021.
Identifiers: LCCN: 2020923713 | ISBN: 978-1-7355523-3-0 (Hardcover) |
978-1-9559750-3-2 (pbk.) | 978-1-7355523-7-8 (pbk.) | 978-1-7355523-9-2 (ebook)
Subjects: LCSH Poetry, American. | American poetry--21st century. | Emotions--Poetry. |
African Americans--Poetry. | Love poetry, American. | BISAC POETRY / American /
General | POETRY / American / African American | POETRY / Subjects & Themes / Death,
Grief, Loss | POETRY / Subjects & Themes / Love & Erotica
Classification: LCC PS3623.E4698 L66 2021 | DDC 811/.6--dc23

First Edition 2021
Jacket design by Jordan Wells

Art illustration Copyright © 2021 by Jordan Wells

For special inquiries, please email us at scottandscholarspress@yahoo.com
Printed in the United States of America

10 9 8 7 6 5 4 3 2 1

Contents

I would like to dedicate this book to all of you who have ever been in love, but it did not work out. You are not alone; a better, healthier love awaits you.

Introduction

I could not stay away for too long. I have returned for a fourth time. For my readers who have been reading my work since the first book, "*Logged Off: My Journey of Escaping the Social Media World*," I do this for you, and you are forever appreciated. Much love and respect to you. You have been loyal to all four of my books. You know what that tells me? That tells me that I have made somewhat of an impact in your life. That tells me that you will continue to support my creative writing ventures. That means the absolute world to me. It gives me such purpose, a sincere purpose to get better at my writing craft, to create new stories and visionary poetry.

Now, for those of you who are new to my work, I would like to welcome you personally, through this introduction of course. I would like to say thank you very much for given my work a chance. You may have never heard of me before, so I thought it would be great to welcome you and to thank you. I hope you enjoy the journey I have prepared for you.

So, here we are, in the year 2021. We made it! By the grace of God, we made it through the year of 2020. What a year; 2020, a year that will take some time to heal from. For me, it was a bittersweet year for me. It was the year of so many tragedies. So many lives lost from the Covid-19 pandemic, an extremely tense presidential election, quarantining, and family and friends separated for long periods of time. While all of that happened, I wrote and published my first three books.

I was a very busy man this past year, even under all of that madness. On top of all of that, I was not on social media. I deleted all of my accounts back in 2018. If you already read *"Logged Off,"* you would understand why I did what I had to do. So, I definitely kept myself busy during the stay-at-home orders.

But my God, what a year that was. I am just glad I am doing well; I am glad my family is doing well, and I am glad you are doing well. We survived that year, which is why I am grateful for every day I am blessed with. But anyways, I do not want you to dwell on any of that in this book. 2020 is over now. This is a new year, with a new book.

In this new book, "*A Lonely Rose*," this particular poetry book is going to be different from my other poetry books "*Mirrors and Reflections*" and "*The Healing*." In this book, I will be limiting such poems that deals with politics, social injustices, racism, or any other controversial statements. In this book, I will focus more on our experiences with love, heartbreak, being single, and perhaps alone. I will touch more on my thoughts and visions of how we deal with love and how disappointing it could become for us.

That will be my focus for this new book. I really just wanted to take a break from the controversial talk. I think after what I said in my third book, "*The Healing*," that was controversial enough. I guess you can say that my mind guided me in this direction. Perhaps because this is my current lifestyle, it is how I feel at this moment in my life.

I guess the only way you will understand how I feel is by me being absolutely honest with you and to tell the truth. The truth is, when it comes to love or being in love, I am a lonely rose. On the book cover, that lonely rose that you see floating in the deep ocean, that represents me. I am that lonely rose. I am just floating away, not sure of where I am going, what my destination will be, and who I will meet.

I feel the only way this book will work is by me living my truth. The only way you as the reader will connect with any of these stories, is by me telling my truth and living my truth. My truth is that in my whole life, as of now, I have only been in love once. I never experienced an authentic, long-term relationship. Why, some of you may be asking? Because I was selfish with my time. I was young and whatever time I dedicated to women, was time wasted. Well, maybe that is not as accurate. I should say I misused the time. I guess I should say that I took some things for granted, and my opportunities got away.

I missed a few opportunities and when I tried to recreate that feeling with women, it was too late. It was too late, and nothing worked out. Did I take it well? No, of course not. I took it like a spoiled, immature brat. I learned many lessons and gained many blessings.

It is so funny, because I, for the most part remember every woman I have ever dated, was interested in, as well as the one I fell in love with. I got along with most of them. A few I just met once, and that was it. Some years ago, a woman I went on a date with, I saw her once again at a store. I said hello to her, but she did not remember me, or maybe she pretended to not remember, who knows, right? If she did not remember me, I am kind of glad because we had a fall out and ended things on bad terms.

I met some interesting women in my life. I actually had a woman completely cut me off after one date; can you guess why? No, it was not because I treated her badly. It was because I do not drink alcohol. When I told her that I do not drink, she looked at me as if she saw a ghost. After I told her, she kind of zoned out during our date. I guess I did not understand how important alcohol is to people's lives.

I have also met with women who I have talked to briefly, great conversations, and then out of nowhere, they just go ghost. It is so weird, so strange. But hey, no one owes anyone an explanation these days. People just cut you off and that is it. It came to a point where I stopped looking for love, I stopped looking to date, and I gave up. I know that is not the way to go by it. But in today's world, to find someone who is worthwhile, with the temptation of social media, you really cannot have expectations, and that goes for people of any age.

But as I said before, I must live my truth, and truthfully, I have become a lonely rose. I replaced dates with work, trying to put a blind eye to my wants and needs. It worked sometimes, but some days, it does get to me. There were times I would blame myself for why things did not work out with certain women I was involved with. But then I had to snap out of that and stop blaming myself. I had to say to myself, "what is meant for me, will be."

The concept of the rose, it was inspired by one of my favorite poets, The late, great Tupac Amaru Shakur. His poetry book, *"The Rose That Grew from Concrete,"* I compare myself to that rose that Tupac talked about in his poem. Beautiful, fragile, but very strong. I compare myself to that rose, I grew from concrete. But unfortunately, I am a lonely rose. Now let me be clear, there is a difference between loneliness and desperation. In no way am I saying I am a desperate person. Sometimes we are dealt a certain hand of cards in life, and the odds are against you.

I am not hurting; I have been healing, I handle things better when situations do not work out with women. Spiritually I am in a good place, and I am at peace. But to be honest, it does get lonely at times. Plus, I am still young, I started the new chapter of my life, which is my thirties. I look forward to it, with great ambition.

What is interesting is that I have dated and conversated with women from all different walks of life. Women of different nationalities, different ethnicities, and you know what they all have in common? They are human beings, who have their flaws and imperfections. Which helps me with lowering my standards and expectations with women. Also, it helps me to be patient with women as well.

Let me just say this, it is very important that you love yourself. Do not make it other people's responsibility to love you or make you happy. Some people out there barely love themselves, and if they barely love themselves, how could they possibly expect to love other people, or for other people to love them? As cliché as it sounds, you have to love yourself. Yes, it may be a lonely road at first, but it will make you stronger to deal with reality, and you will be able to see yourself in the mirror and love that person that you see.

But on a positive note, because I always look at the bright side of things. Being alone allowed me to focus on my work, and make it happen. Again, I wrote and published three books in one year alone. You are now reading my fourth, and by the time you read this, I will already be writing my fifth book. Now if I was in a relationship, when would I have the time to sit down and create all of this poetry, all of these stories? What if I was married with children? I wouldn't have the time to write all of this, I would be busy taking care of my family. I have the freedom to do what I do, to live my life for me, and that is one of the benefits of being alone. So, it is not always a bad thing, if you are ever alone, use that time wisely to get things done. To live your life for you, to find yourself, your purposes, and build a legacy that could possibly last forever.

But with all of that being said, these stories I have prepared for you, some will strongly relate to you, and others will be for pure entertainment. Many will be fictional, like all of my works. I just want for you, the reader, to enjoy these poems and short stories. I do not want you to feel sorry for me, in any way. I understand that love will come. The real, true love will come, and by that time, I will be much more prepared mentally, physically, and spiritually, and I will appreciate her. Now, I present to you, "*A Lonely Rose.*"

But before you start, I must give you a fair warning about some of the content in this book. In these fictional short stories, "*Charli's Chance*" and "*The Forbidden Lake,*" there are some pretty graphic depictions, foul adult language, talks of sexual assault, sexually explicit content, and graphic imagery of horror. Also, there is a poem called "*Little Jewish Boy in the Ghetto,*" that is based on a fictional child, but talks about the real tragic events of the Holocaust. The poem contains some graphic imagery, that may not be suitable for everyone. But to be absolutely clear, in no way am I trying to make light of such a horribly tragic, unforgettable event. I feel that it is important that people do not forget such events that happened in history. So, I wanted to create a story, based on true events, in honor of those who lost their lives, and their families.

Prelude

Truth and Lies

The truth; tell me the truth. What is the truth? Do we know what the truth is? Do we even care about the truth? Is the truth as popular as the lies are? What is truth? What are lies? I took a look at the definitions of the words "truth and lies," and I find them very interesting. I will just give you a few definitions of each; for the word "truth," it says, *"conformity; fact; actuality, the state or character of being true."* As for "lie," it says, *"false statement; with deliberate intent to deceive; an intentional untruth; inaccurate."*

So, when I looked up the definitions of both words "truth and lie," I try to connect them with people, and how people use both truth and lies in their everyday lives. I would say we have all told a truth at some point in our lives, and we have all lied before. Do not read this and deliberately "lie" to yourself and say that you have never told a lie a day in your life. No one is perfect; I have told the truth many times as well as told many lies. I try my best to tell the truth and live my truth, more than lying to people. After a while, the lies grow out of control, and you become mentally enslaved to lies.

Lying never really worked for me. It really is a sound thing. To lie to someone and be believable, that requires some talent. I believe with this whole new world of technology; people cannot get away with lying as much as we once did. There are just way too many eyes on you with social media, and you have to come with those receipts.

Now, you may be thinking, what does the truth and lies have to do with this particular poetry book? What does this have to do with "*A Lonely Rose*?" Well, have you ever been in a relationship or dated someone? Have you ever told them a lie, or you have been lied to? I cannot answer that for you, but just ask yourself. I most definitely have. I have told lies to women before, just as I know they have lied to me.

Denial is always at the tip of ones' tongue. There was a time I was dealing with a woman, she told me that she could not make it and had to cancel our date because she had a lot going on. At that time, I was on social media. When I looked at my Instagram news feed, I saw that same woman flirting with another guy, asking him, "so, when are we going out?" I find it hilarious; I would just be saying to myself, "why people cannot be honest and just tell the truth?" If you are not interested in someone, just be upfront with it. These days people get left on "read" via text message, people cut you off, and it goes back to what I said in my first book, "*Logged Off: My Journey of Escaping the Social Media World*." In that book, I said that we are now living in this new era of streaming. Not only are we streaming music services, tv shows, movies, and podcast. We are now streaming friendships, relationships, and politics. You could be in a relationship today, engaged even; two months later, you broke it off. There's so much temptation out there. It is extremely challenging for people to be honest, with themselves, and with other people.

I believe the truth and the lies are within all of us. We cannot help ourselves; again, we are only human. Sometimes we tell lies, just so we do not hurt someone. Some people cannot handle what the truth is. The truth is the gun and lies are the bullets. Like a gun, if you cannot handle the truth properly, you are going to let off some lies and hurt people.

Better yet, I would say that the truth is a pimp and lies are the hoes. Lies are very deceiving, they make you feel good, the lies tell you what you want to hear. The truth is very difficult to get a hold of. The truth does not want to be discovered or exposed. So, the truth pimps the lies to us, and yes, those lies definitely entertains us. That is the game; people do not really care about hearing the truth. Feed them the lies and they will consume; they will feed the machines big money.

Are you still with me so far? Have I lost you? Go ahead and take a moment to process all of what I just said up to this point. Seriously, take a moment, look up and just process what I said. Oh, and if you looked up and saw that the time was 11:11, make a wish.

Okay, now let's get back to it. This is what we have to deal with, in our lives as people. We deal with truth and lies. Again, no one is perfect. We all have had our share of lies and telling the truth and living our truth. I strongly believe that it is crucial that we maintain a healthy balance of truth and lies. Just like with my work; I can tell you the truth right now and say that I wrote all four of my books. But I would be lying to you if I said absolutely no one has influenced me or inspired me to write these books. I would be completely lying to you if I said I had no inspiration from life itself, to write the poems and short stories that I wrote in all four books.

We tend to let some lies slide when people tell them to us. I am sure you have met someone in life, who has lied straight to your face, and you knew they were lying to you, but you let it slide. You may have also lost a lot of respect for that person. But again, no one is perfect, we have had our friends, family, associates lie to us, and vice versa.

The moral of the story is you cannot feed off of the lies that people give you, and still be able to live your truth. Do you understand me? Yes, I know I have to elaborate on this one right here. What I mean is remove yourself from the "Yes Men" and "Yes Women." Remove yourself from people who do not give a damn about you, who are going to continuously feed you lies, just to please your ears, and not keep it real with you.

Heaven forbid, but if you were falling ill, and the doctor kept telling you, "oh, you are okay, you are fine, or you look better than ever," and you believed that doctor, but then later realized your health is actually on a decline. That is what I mean by you not living your truth and you are being fed lies. To live your truth is to protect who you are in this world. To be unapologetic about who you are and love who you are.

Yes, you may feel lonely at times when you live your truth, like a lonely rose. But it is so worth it. Lies are not your friend, they are enablers. As I said, people at times will tell you the truth, but they will also feed you lies. But it is up to you to decide when you have had enough of the bullshit that people try to force feed to you, and for you to remove yourself from that toxic energy.

But yea, I think I have made my point with all of that. Just accept the fact that we all have to deal with truth and lies. There is no escaping it, you can only hope to maintain the balance. Sometimes when it comes to the truth, you do not always get the whole truth. You only get bits and pieces of it, and when you put two and two together, you put those puzzle pieces in the right position, and you see the clearer picture, the truth will then set you free, and you will finally have some closure and some healing. Just like I said in my third book, "*The Healing,*" you cannot find healing without the truth.

But pardon me; that was just me venting and giving my take on what I feel about truth and lies. Feel free to disagree with me, or maybe you agree. It is something to think about. But with all of that being said, you are definitely going to see a lot of lies and some truth within these poems.

So, the first poem I will present is a special one. I do not know if you the reader can relate to this story, but I figured it would be an entertaining one to start you off with. It is a poem called "*The Marriage That Didn't Happened.*"

The Marriage That Didn't Happened (09/24/20 12:41a.m.)

Up with the birds, a special day for a special man,

He's about to walk down the aisle, a special wedding has

been planned.

Ten minutes away from him, is his gorgeous bride to be,

A bachelorette party she won't forget, but looking in the

mirror, happiness is not what she sees.

She slowly makes her way to bathe, her hair's tangled with

drought,

Cold feet in a hot shower, she's drowning in doubt.

The shower can barely keep up, tear drops fall from her eyes,

She can't go through with this, "I do" will be nothing but a

lie.

He knows nothing of her doubts, he's ready to make her his

wife,

Little does he know that the wedding cake will not be cut

today, no need for a knife.

He shaved, he showered, groomsmen are all ready to go,

She's stalling, hasn't done her make up, she's ready to say

no.

She breaks down in front of her bridesmaids, asking them to

keep this a secret,

She's said, "I can't do this, I can't go forward with this future

regret."

They tell her she must face him, only the truth can set her free,

She said, "I can't hurt him, if I do this, he'll hate me."

He arrives at the wedding, friends and family are there,

Her makeup is set, almost done with her hair,

As she sits, an unhappy face in the mirror, a regretful stare.

She can't take it anymore, she calls him on his phone,

It's dialing, it's dialing; but he doesn't hear it, muted ringtone.

A voicemail she leaves him, but didn't say she's leaving him,

She said, "I have to talk to you, it's a very important reason."

Her phone rings, her sweaty palm picks up and hears his voice,

He said, "it's bad luck to speak before we wed, but I didn't like the sound of your voice."

She told him, "I have to speak to you, face to face,"

He responded, "name the place."

They finally meet; a quiet lake, just the two,

He's in his tuxedo, but she's not in her dress, I guess she won't be saying, "I do."

He says, "you're so beautiful, you would look even more beautiful in your dress,"

She responded, "I've been going through it this morning, under a lot of stress."

He said, "why? What's going through your mind?"

She's speechless; looking for the honest words to say, but they're so hard to find.

He walks to her and holds both her hands,

She's about to spill the beans; like roots, she hopes he understands.

He tells her, "Everyone is waiting, we really should go,"

He walks while he holds her hand, she doesn't budge, and answer is no.

He's not putting two and two together, he's facing a heartbreak,

She looks him in his eyes and said, "today, no one is cutting the wedding cake."

He looked at her for so long, it felt like an hour,

She said, "I felt I was making a huge mistake, ever since my bridal shower."

He turned away from her, teary eyes gazing at the lake,

He asked her, "so none of this was real? It was all fake?"

She told him, "Love is so strange,

One minute you have it close to you, then later on it's out of range."

He turned with the quickness and said, "what's that supposed to mean?"

She said, "I lost my feelings for you, but I'm not trying to be mean."

She walked towards him with a fist; he said, "so now you're
going to take a swing?"
She opened her hand and gave back the diamond ring.
Tears going down the aisles of her face,
Both hearts disqualified from this pre-martial race.
She looks up at him, no apology has ever been more sincere,
She gave him a kiss goodbye, and a whisper in his ear.
Whatever she said to him, it put a smile on his face,
A duet stare, a duet comment, "anytime, anyplace."
He decided to leave, while she stayed,
Looking out at the lake, she closed her eyes and prayed.
She said, "dear God, I didn't feel it, it wasn't fate,
But I know you know what you're doing, so I'm going to
wait."

A Soul I Once Still Loved (09/22/20 9:20 p.m.)

I pledged allegiance to her, honored her spirit,

Her voice is absent to my senses, only memories grant my

wishes to hear it.

I miss giving her kisses to her smiling cheek,

I hated my ego, my jealousy made me weak.

One argument too many, I disobeyed her trust,

I was dedicated to fear, submissive to lust.

As if I was paying homage to a coward,

I let a prior heartbreak take control, it became empowered.

Perhaps I broke her heart and didn't even know it,

Maybe she was too proud, or too hurt to even show it.

I never got to tell her I love her, now it is too late,

Another presence of a man is active, perhaps he's her

soulmate.

I was young, not trying to make alibis,

But I did, I did get to tell her goodbye.

But I just want to say hello again,

And ask her, "when, where, and why did it end?"

How did we break up before we even connected?

A blunt rejection, so unexpected,

This was a body of mystery, too late to dissect it.

How do you still love someone when it never reached that

finish line?

I just want to recreate the past, one more kiss, one more time.

I hope she reads this one day, by then, she'd probably forgot me,

Erased my name, erased my voice, remembers nothing about me.

I can accept that; I shed no more tears,

A man that treats her with disrespect is all that I fear.

Heartbreak is heartbreaking to live with, but as always, I survive,

I found my healing, I just look in the mirror and say, "you're too alive."

Connected Complexions (09/22/20 7:44 p.m.)

A complexion with melanin, 5'4 was her height,

Blind date in effect; this should be an interesting night.

A man comes her way, he stands at 6'3,

His complexion is much lighter, but darker than a white tee.

He says hello to her, and asked if she's his blind date,

She said yes with glazing eyes, staring at her drop-dead
gorgeous soulmate.

She knew he was the one during this dinner for two,

Thinking in her mind, "this is just too good to be true."

He complimented her looks, tells her she's beautiful,

Three course meal, a couple drinks spill, no dessert, they're
pretty full.

Two different complexions, holding hands, making a
connection,

She feels so comfortable with him, he gives her protection.

Walking by a pier, they hold each other through a chilly
breeze,

They take a selfie together, smile for the gram; "say cheese!"

Likes and comments; some good, some were bad,

One comment said, "you look great together," another; I can't
say, it's so sad.

What year is this again? So what if they don't have the same
complexion,

We're trying to kill racism, while ignorance is giving it
resurrection.
They began to stare at each other, her brown eyes looking
into his eyes of crystal-clear blue,
Holding each other so tight, as if they were stuck like glue.
She stood on her tippy toes, eyes closed for the kiss,
A feeling she's never felt before, a mocha chocolate-vanilla
twist.
But this is not ice cream, these are two human beings,
Falling in love with each other, she said, "my God, it feels
like I'm dreaming."
She gently caresses his groomed five o' clock shadowed face,
Two different complexions making their mark to change the
human race.
They planned their second date, no more blind eyes,
They said their good nights; a hug, a kiss, then began to sigh.
Connected complexions; don't judge, don't hate,
Maybe it is you who should go on a blind date.

You're My Everything <small>(09/22/20 5:46 p.m.)</small>

You're my contemporary, you're my past,

You're my first, you're my last.

You're my love making, you're my porn,

You're my halo, you're my horns.

You're my focus, you're my distraction,

You're my confrontation, you're my reaction.

You're my poster, you're my movie,

You're my stillness, yet you move me.

You're my shower, you're my rain,

You're my pleasure, you're my pain.

You're my calm, you're my anger,

You're my safety, you're my danger.

You're my inbox, you're my sent,

You're my devil who wears Prada, yet you're a heaven sent.

You're my welcome, you're my leave,

You're my lies, you're what I believe.

You're my smoke, you're my fire,

You're my streets, you're my tires.

You're my stress, you're my test,

You're my worst, you're my best.

You're my easy, you're my hard,

You're my first day of school, you're my last report card.

You're my birth, you're my death,

You're my first word, you're my last breath.

Damn; you really are my everything,

Damn; you really are everything,

Damn; you really everything,

Damn; you everything,

Damn everything,

Damn.

Marley   (10/09/20 1:40 a.m.)

Jah Rastafari is what he speaks in the microphone,

With a revolutionary voice, a militant tone.

He closes his eyes and begins to sing,

A deep crease between his eyebrows, watch as his dreadlocks

swing.

The magic; watching him dance on the stage,

Feeding the hungry audience with information, getting his

people on the same page.

The melodies: his guitar was his instrumental gun,

It wasn't always about WAR, just put on "One Love," and

let's have some fun.

But some did not find him fun, but a dangerous man,

A shot in the dark, a target for a political assassination plan.

He was too resilient, back on stage he goes,

A growing family he had, more children, more shows.

He was his people's leader, emancipating them with

harmonic communication,

Interviewers asked him about the herb, he said, "it is the

healing of the nation."

A growing pain in his toe, but pays it no mind,

The pain then metastasizes, from his toe to his mind.

But he didn't stop, kept liberating his people, performing on

stage,

Until the pain crossed him over to the Almighty; a legend,
thirty-six years of age.
The echo of his essence resonates through his children,
granddaughters, and grandsons,
A new generation of Marley, the music has just begun.
Ture peace and love were all he asked, all he gave,
Free your mind, don't be a slave.
His music and legacy lives on every day and every night,
Don't forget his words, "Get up, stand up, stand up for your
right!"

The Poem   (10/23/20 3:02p.m.)

Politics, go away for good,

Voters contemplating whether or not they could,

Very few are hesitant about if they should.

Love is very ill, no treatment during this pandemic,

Children staring at screens all day long, barely able to keep

up with their academics.

This virus; trying to come into every home like it's Santa

Claus,

Are you a Demo or a Repub? Hard to stick with your pick,

both has black and blue flaws.

Guns are what people blame, but bullets we ignore,

Taxes scaring off the rich but crucifying the poor.

Lies and fake news, where's the receipts,

Face masks and happy hour, social distancing seats.

Still hearing sneezes, no longer hearing "God Bless you,"

The number of cases are still growing, but don't let it stress you.

Sports are the new illusion, Rest in Peace to the games,

Celebrating trophies without the fans, sports will never be the

same.

Warning after warning; fake news becomes true cries,

They're not going to be satisfied until millions die.

So many cases, limited hospital places,

No more love at first sight, can't see anyone's faces.

Is there a finish line to this madness,

Is there happiness after this sadness?

Are there any answers after the smoke clears,

Any smiles left after all the tears?

I don't know, I don't know, haven't got a clue,

In case no one has asked you in so long, how are you?

Couple's Corruption

(10/24/20 12:52 a.m.)

Where's the trust in them?

He blames her, she blames him.

Neither has the truth to give,

The lies and lies they constantly relive.

The lies and cries he stains her heart with,

Her lies are too perfect, so believable, she has a gift.

She has the unstoppable questions, yet he returns no answers,

He tries to interrogate, but he has no chance with her.

They don't want to break up, yet they both cheat,

So conflicting and oh so bittersweet.

Until the day he had enough,

When she became physical with him, a bit rough.

He said, "keep your hands to yourself,"

Scratching away at his skin, his morals, and his mental
health.

She kept swinging towards his face,

If he were to swing in return, he knows he'll lose this case.

His hands stay down, yet hers are swinging in midair,

Breaking her nails after every punch, she just doesn't care.

A toxic relationship is coming to a much-needed finish line,

He must walk away swiftly before this becomes an abusive
crime.

He succeeded, her broken fingers came together in handcuffs,

He made some favorable choices as he said, "enough is enough."
But no matter how you see this, neither were saints,
Neither had good intentions, both filled with unforgivable taint.
Can you relate to this? I sure hope not,
This was destined to die, let it rot.

Learning, Earning, Burning (10/24/20 1:50 a.m.)

Nightmares never die when you die in those streets,

Running from the "policense and registrations," they're so

cold with the heat.

Drug dealing on the block,

The only product that's never out of stock.

Protest became the photo op,

War has begun with the cops.

Pandemic didn't stop the movement,

Sickness in the air, where's the hugs, the love, where it went?

Politicians saying, "pick me, pick me,"

COVID-19 made them like, "sick me, sick me."

No mask, no mercy; this is not a game,

Conspiracy theories; trying to vaccinate our veins,

DNA enslavement is coming, they are coming for our brains.

I'm learning; I learned that Hitler wasn't the biggest monster,

History didn't mention Léopold II of Belgium, that was the

devil's ultimate sponsor.

You explore and you learn,

You give and you earn,

Test the fire but let nothing burn,

Be patient, wait your turn,

Watch for phonies when the tables turn,

Until next time, I need to adjourn.

"As you get older, you begin to wisely show the world who you are, confidently, and also know the purposes you can confidently offer to the world."

A Gangster's Perception   (10/24/20 2:36 a.m.)

I can't tell you how many times I heard the devil laughing at
night,

The gun shots always outnumbered the normal fist fights.

Soldiers with a vengeance, trying to change their mind,

They can't hear what I'm saying, can't see, illegally blind.

Too much youth in the streets, I want them out for good,

But where can they go when all they know is the hood?

Young wild child on the corners, ready to blast for me,

They don't believe in God, living with deep blasphemy.

Blast for me with minor catastrophe,

Running out of cemetery space, no casket for me.

The drug game never had winners,

Just poisoners and killing sinners.

Money came in while dope fiends came out, dead,

So many young boys laying on the concrete bed, dead,

A bullet in his head before the knowledge he could've read.

Prison profits have risen, innocent criminals,

Going away for maximum time, for charges that were so
minimal.

Justice is the beautiful woman that got away,

Every time I "DM" her, she leaves me on read every day.

The news always says good morning but have bad news,

They don't call it bad; they call it fake, believe what you
choose.

A bullet doesn't have a name on it,

But it definitely does have aim on it,

Spark the flame, babies catch the pain on it,

Mommas closing more caskets, placing flowers on it.

Just a different brother,

Didn't get to say goodbye to his mother.

The shooters are just looters who steal life,

Married to the gun; it's their steel wife.

Bullets are the kids they abandoned, expecting another man to
take them into custody of his flesh,

The stress of broken families stays oh so fresh.

Gangsters don't make room for holidays,

They just say hallelujah for making it another day.

Is there any way out of the madness, the devil doesn't want
me to leave,

Praying to win in life, but the devil doesn't want me to
believe.

He wants me to stay and become his demon,

Stay a slave while I'm fighting hard for my freedom.

I want out of this curse,

Those same followers on the gram aren't going to be
following your hearse.

No more court cases,

No more police chases,

No more buck-fifty faces,

Goodness gracious.

Goodness gracious,

Tired of these racists,

They're trying to erase us.

Maybe the world's gone mad and I cared to join,

One day money will be no more, stunting with bitcoins.

"The only nightmare that I have is waking up from a good dream, and you're not lying next to me to tell you about it."

Murder After Midnight   (10/25/20 9:12 a.m.)

A skinny dip; ten minutes after twelve o'clock at night,

The babysitter hears commotion next door, sounds like a big
fight.

She continues to swim, pays it no more attention,

Her neglect is her future regret of no prevention.

The babysitter steps up out of the pool,

Her nude body dripping wet, bathrobe on the stool.

She covers up and wraps the straps around her waist,

She's a bit curious about the argument next door, but her time
she doesn't want to waste.

She goes up the stairs to check on the sleeping toddlers,

They are counting everlasting sheep; she noticed the toddler's
binoculars.

She grabbed them with curiosity, scoping around next door,

What her two eyes saw through those lens, she never saw
before.

She saw a woman's body; blood splattered all over the walls,

In shock, her hands are shivering in terror, the binoculars
took a breaking fall.

She panics, saying "oh my god," covering her mouth with her
shaking hand,

Her instant regret for not calling the cops beforehand.

Rushed to her phone, called the parents with cussing urgency,

But the prancing parents delivered no answer, then she text,
"please call, it's an emergency,"
Then she called the cops, dispatcher asked, "what is the
emergency?"
The babysitter said, "Someone's been murdered, please come
now,"
She gets the common questions of who, what, when, where,
and how.
In the middle of the law enforcement conversation, she hears
the sound of the doorbell,
If you could see the frightening pose, her night has become a
living hell.
She slowly walks down the stairs, there's another doorbell
ring,
Only in the bathrobe, completely naked, not even a G-string.
She looks at the doorbell camera, no one is there,
She opens the door, nothing but the chilly wind blowing her
frizzled hair.
She received a gently touch from behind, she screamed as if
she was in a horror video,
She looked down and saw the toddler and said, "oh, it's just
you kiddo."
The little boy asked, "what's wrong?"
She didn't tell him, just rushed him upstairs and sang the
"twinkle, twinkle" song.

A LONELY ROSE

She saw the time "1:11" on the toddler's clock,

She then realized that she left the front door unlocked.

She hurries down swiftly and turns that lock,

Five minutes later, she hears a knock.

She didn't bother to look at the camera, because it was a
knock, and not a ring,

Big mistake as she opens the door, a quick slash to her arm, a
bleeding sting.

It was the killer from next door, coming to kill another,

All she thought in that split second was that she's never again
going to see her mother.

Another sharp swing, but this time the killer failed,

As she tried to run, the killer grabbed the bathrobe strap, like
a wolf grabbing a sheep's tail.

She manages to escape the bathrobe, now she's dressed only
in her blood, sweat and tears,

She gets away from the killer, but the killer reaching the kids
it what she fears.

Her heart's racing from 0 to 100; it's on overdrive,

She then hears sirens, red and blue flickering, the cops have
arrived.

The killer disappeared, bloody bathrobe left on the floor,

She grabs it and covers herself, waiting for the cops at the
front door.

Teardrops melting down on her face, the cops look in disbelief,

She said, "the killer attacked me," as the cops began to debrief.

She finally gets a call from the parents, asking her if everything's okay,

She said, "absolutely not, come home right away."

She gets dressed and stitched up, now holding the toddlers tight,

Thinking to herself, "this has been one hell of an evil night."

The killer is still on the loose, trauma running through her veins,

Cops carrying on with their questions, details after details, they need names.

She tells them, "I'm just a babysitter, I don't know the neighbors next door,

I heard arguments earlier, but minded my business, and didn't bother."

It all sounds like such a scary movie, poor thing,

Now she may scream every time she hears a doorbell ring.

She may never be the same again, a terrifying feeling,

Until that killer is caught, she will never find her healing.

Work Ethic   (10/4/20 4:38 a.m.)

It's hard to sleep with women when you don't sleep,

I count my blessing instead of counting sheep.

Up at the wee hours writing my gift,

To help the masses, to inspire, to uplift.

My brain won't stop, how can I?

I don't want to miss a thought or idea; I'll sleep when I die.

I'm listening to Ye, he said get your ass up and intellectually

grind,

Create your dreams, you're too brilliant of a mind.

I missed out on parties, missed a lot of dates,

Four books in a year, lots of marketing and promo rates.

I love it, they are my babies, my truth,

From trees to paper, my written thoughts grow with brain cell

roots.

It's 4 am and I'm not sleepy,

Where are these words coming from, it's so creepy.

Like a bunch of spirits in my mind, giving me ideas,

It's all in what I see, what I feel, and what I hear.

I just write, and write, and write, I'm bleeding,

I'm texting these words in my notes, auto correct and

deleting.

808s and Heartbreak; my go to inspiration,

I hear sounds, see colors, a vision of civilization.

Staring at my ceiling like it's a brand-new canvas,

It's hard to explain, the visions I have to see through, please understand this.

It's not about the money, okay I lie,

No, I lie again, it's not, but I hope you continue to buy.

Alone in The Night   (09/26/20 1:00 a.m.)

Dried tears, a wet stain on his pillowcase,

Lying in bed, missing his wife's enchanted face.

The arguments, the yelling, uncontrollable screams,

His insomnia puts caffeine to shame, no need for dreams.

She's on his mind, dancing on every brain cell,

He's obsessed with her, must be a curse, an enchanted spell.

She hasn't called, it's been over week,

Staring at his phone, he takes a social media peek,

He sees her out partying, his anxiety reached its peak,

His assumptions grow heavy while his heart grows weak.

Alone; he needs her, wants her in his arms,

He's looking at their picture together, the same picture she
wears as a necklace charm.

He slowly slips into a much-needed rest,

Morning comes; she is there, laying her head on his bare
chest.

He embraced her, held her like there was no tomorrow,

Kissed her with sincerity, with love and much sorrow.

He said, "don't ever leave me again, you're all I have left in
my heart,"

She kissed him and said, "we will always have our ups and
downs, but it's always and forever, til death do us part."

"Love always says goodbye, leaving behind inherited pain."

She Left (09/26/20 1:00 a.m.)

Hard to let go, the pain is never fun,

She told me I wasn't the one,

We weren't on the same page, and now that chapter is done.

I lie to myself, telling myself I don't need her,

I just want her back, when my heart breaks, I bleed her.

I never had lips like hers imprinted on my flesh,

A head full of hair gently planted on top of my chest.

Memories of her, they faded away like a split-second dream,

The voice of her, I can't hear it like a deep ocean scream.

She's gone, settled in love with another guy,

I would say I don't love her anymore, my God, what a lie,

I couldn't stop loving her even if I try.

I look up at the sky while thinking of her, it gives me peace,

All the lessons learned, she had to teach.

I didn't always have the answers, that was true,

I longed for her; she was the dream I wanted to pursue.

But failure came to be, and I had to accept my leave,

I may never see her in this life again, it's hard to believe,

Falling in love is like falling leaves,

Its seasoned, like colored trees.

"Real estate has become the gentrified soldiers looking to wipe out the average living people."

The Devil in Heels (10/7/20 9:18 p.m.)

The most beautiful figure a woman could ever be,

Poisonous to the core, but her seduction is cure to man's misery.

A man comes her way, he asked for her name,

She whispered in his ear and said, "it's Luci, let's play a game."

He said, "it's nice to meet you Luci, what game shall we play?"

She responded, "it's at my home, take me there, it's only 13 minutes away."

They leave the country club, leaving in his car,

Little does he know that her heart is as black as tar.

Evil never looked so beautiful in an all-black dress, 6-inch heels,

He's dressed to impressed, and she's dressed to kill.

13 minutes exactly, a two-story mansion is where she resides,

She tells him the game has begun; it's called "don't call it a suicide."

He grows worried, not sure about what he's got himself into,

Not sure if she's sane or a bit mental.

But he's already possessed, she draws him in the house,

A black cat is about to go hunting for an innocent white mouse.

Off with the lights, she leaves him in darkness and silence,

He calls her name, sparks a flame, she's a woman of
wickedness and violence.

He said, "this isn't funny Luci, I'm about to leave,"

She then appears and says, "I just want to play a little Adam
and Eve."

She didn't give him an apple, but the heart of a goat,

His eyes grow terrified as she put a knife against his throat.

"Bite the heart," is what she said with her demon eyes,

He looked in her eyes and realized the devil is alive.

He bit the heart, blood drops began to stain the ground,

Blurry visions, his stomach makes disturbing sounds.

He's losing consciousness as he crawls his way to the door,

But she drags him back, as his body mops the blood off the
floor.

Down her dungeon he goes, shackled and tossed in a cage,

He sees that there are others, other men, all on the same
satanic page.

As he gains his consciousness, he asked the others, "who the
hell is she?"

They said, "Ms. Diablo, number six, in a pair of three."

The man asked, "We have to escape her,"

Hesitating as they said, "it's not her; it's, it's Lucifer."

The Missing   (10/28/20 5:48 p.m.)

We move forward in this rotating pebble,

Looking for answers we will never find, we're rebels.

What is the Moon, the deserts of the earth,

What is death, what is life, what is birth?

What is missing from our everyday lives,

Loved ones passing away, day by day, nine to five.

We miss this friend, miss that friend,

We make our broken promises saying, "friends until the end."

Until one friend's end is sooner than expected,

Too late for forgiveness, can't be resurrected.

Missed out on opportunities, missed out on love,

A true love that you could be proud of, a gift you walked out

of.

Missing is the mother that gives birth to the children of

regrets,

All the wasted time I spent surfing the internet.

We are a species of the missed,

A decline of hugs, not all of us have been properly kissed.

I miss friends, I miss family, but I don't want to miss myself,

Spending too much time thinking of others, I don't want to

miss out on self-wealth.

I don't want to miss too much,

I don't believe in friends through a screen, nothing tangible to

touch.

We take for granted the seeds we haven't yet planted,

We rob the planet of its seeds and take it for granted.

We're missing out on the beauty of nature,

We must beg nature for forgiveness, we must chase her.

You've missed enough, put down the phone,

Create a better life, a much loving home.

I miss you is growing more and more fake,

"Too busy" is no longer the excuse, Rendezvous now for

goodness sake.

Scream Humans, Scream   (10/30/20 12:00 a.m.)

Streets still flooded with RIP's,

Baby boys with lethal toys and smartphones, say cheese.

Rats love cheese, they're flooding the streets too,

Rap is the new political party, but did they bite off more than

they can chew?

Hachew! Hachew! Was that a sneeze? God bless you,

COVID is... I better not say, don't want to stress you.

So confusing, the truth is missing,

Lies going live, caskets receiving heavy kissing.

I just want to scream,

What is this nightmare, this bubble, this dream?

Poverty and debt, black versus white,

We're not colors, enough with this racial fight.

Come together, it's better for the weather,

Stay back, COVID has migrated; the new settler.

Our hatred towards each other put to the test; six feet apart,

Can't see friends and family; that love is seeping out our

hearts.

Scream for mercy, for peace, for justice,

Begging with allegiance to God, but can God trust us?

I don't know, I don't know,

Children come, children grow,

Children learn and graduate, but jobs run slow.

Their stomachs filled with college debt,

Hunting for jobs while behind their ears, they're still a little
wet.

I just want to scream,

Capitalism; death gives birth to live streams.

Bad news gets more views,

They hate the winners, but love it when you lose,

What a sickness; the jealousy flu.

What about you? Do you want to scream? Give it a try,

Take a deep breath and let it fly.

It's okay, no need to feel ashamed,

Too many pointing fingers; a finger-painting game,

Not to worry, God is working overtime to cancel the devil's
flames.

Scream, scream, scream,

Projected voices, what a team.

A dying democracy, or was it ever born?

Morality and integrity, melting in the pot of political scorn.

The freedom of speech,

The absence of leaders, is it too late to teach?

Pastors remote preaching,

Conspiracy theorists reaching,

Democratic text and phone calls; votes beseeching.

I should have answered a call and screamed, saying, "enough
with the phone calls,"

Trump wanted another term; he still wanted to put up the
stone walls.
Scream humans, scream,
Scream wisely.

"Grow fat with money, one eye on the starving peasants."

A Lonely Rose   (10/30/20 1:04 p.m.)

She left me, no goodbyes, no warning, what did I do?

She took her bags, her possessions, she took food too.

I'm starving for answers as to why, why did she leave,

Upset soul, my heartbreak won't allow me to properly

breathe.

I couldn't say I'm sorry, I don't know what I did wrong,

Now here I am, listening to these same old sad songs.

Was there another man that she sees a better life with,

I don't have a clue, life with pain is a cruel bitch.

Was time wasted or was it worthwhile,

Perhaps I didn't provide her desires of a sophisticated

lifestyle.

Yet I don't hate her betrayal, I could understand,

My broken heart bled so much, I left bloody footprints in the

sand.

The sand that imprinted our footprints, her photogenic Kodak

face,

Feels like I'm stuck in a dream, I can't move, she's running,

but I can't chase.

She runs further away from me,

She's screaming, "stay away from me."

Left alone in the dark, in the cold,

Shivering and quivering, my body collapsed, and it fold.

I can't pray to God, the tears won't let me,

My face is all wet, I'm a lonely rose, lost at sea.

Maybe I should drown my hopes, deep into the ocean,

My hopes of another rose with connection, chemistry, such raw emotion.

My peddles are fading and aging, floating away,

The dripping blossom of a rose I am, getting older day by day.

Perhaps I'm just a paranoid person, please, don't mind me,

I'm just a lonely rose, lost at sea.

My Dearest (10/31/20 2:00 p.m.)

So much to tell, but no time to speak,

A love so strong, but the chemistry was so weak.

More than friends, but the engagement had come to an end,

Can't help but cry my hopes of what we could have been.

First we bend, then we broke miles apart,

Long distance faded the bond, I suffered, oh I suffered such a

broken heart.

The thought of you with another, it drove me absolutely

insane,

Nightmares taunting me, having a field day playing tricks in

my brain.

I was angry, with you and with me,

No, perhaps not with you, you just left, but I wasn't ready.

Now I'm alone; stuck with old memories, years too late to

create more,

With just a split-second thought of you, it tingles my core.

Perhaps love is really time and our timing was not right,

I would give anything to once again kiss you goodbye or

even goodnight.

But your lips and cheeks have been consensually invaded by

another man,

Haven't seen your face or compressed our bodies together in

a ten-year span.

But I had to let go, although the memories are still there,

Late night memories of me playing in all that long beautiful

hair.

Your gentle fingers playing with my beard,

Lying in bed now; you're gone, you disappeared.

If time stood still forever, I would want to be still with you,

My dearest; the love I felt with you, it was real, it was true.

She's Only Human (10/31/20 5:00 p.m.)

Still, she hurts; a widow of two years,

Every morning she awakes, her eyes still filled with tears.

Laying in the same bed she once shared with her husband,

Gone so soon, it'll be three years in June, still she doesn't

understand.

Malpractice during surgery, doesn't understand why,

Doctors gave her the bad news, devastated cries,

She collapsed in the waiting room, didn't get a chance to say

goodbye.

Therapist after therapist, they all say the same things,

"You'll find love again, in no time, you'll be wearing a new

engagement ring."

True love is always hard to replace,

Knowing no man in the world will ever have his face.

Except for his older brother; my God, he could be his twin,

Every time she sees him, it's like seeing her husband, from

the outside and within.

What is she thinking, going after her brother in law,

Her desperate attempt to reincarnate her lover, comes with a

consequential flaw.

Her brother in law is already married, her fate may lead to

disaster,

Her plan is to be alone with him, she made a crying call, he couldn't get there any faster,

Oh, what white lies she told, as white as alabaster.

He knocked on her door, he asked her, "what's wrong?"

Her crying face just hugged him, while in the background, she's playing her favorite song.

A song only her husband danced to with her,

I have a feeling that an adulterous night is about to occur.

He held her tight, asking her, "is everything alright?"

She responded, "no, can you please stay for the night?"

He hesitated; gave her a slow horizontal shake of his head,

He said with emotion, "your husband, my brother is dead."

She begged and begged, pleaded for him to stay,

He said, "I'm a married man, and my brother would be turning in his grave,

You will just have to do your best, be strong, be brave."

A hard no could not silence her stubbornness,

She leaned in and gave him a kiss,

Kiss, after kiss, after kiss, after kiss.

His guard began to melt after every kiss,

The more kisses she offered, the more he failed to dismiss.

He kept saying, "stop this; he's gone, he's dead,"

But the clothes kept coming off, eventually they became naked humans, fornicating in bed.

A LONELY ROSE

The same bed she shared with her late husband, a conflicted
romance,

Passionate love making, over and over, sexual abundance.

Both putting their sweat and tears into this sexual race,

Then he ejected his blood line across the finish line of her
fertile place.

Heavily breathing, they gasped for air,

They both give each other an intimate stare,

Rubbing her thumb through his thick beard, while he gently
caressed her dampened hair,

Who would have thought an honest night would turn into a
betraying affair.

What will he tell his wife; secrets are the bones blanketed by
the flesh of lies,

This secret must be taken to the grave, as the truth will only
be rottenly revealed once they die.

Ashes to ashes; dust to dust,

The birth of their child will come, death to the trust.

Don't judge her; she's only human, just like you,

Look in the mirror and ask yourself, "what would you do?"

"The "En" Effect.

First it's the Engagement,

Second is the Entanglement,

Third is the Entitlement,

And then it is the End."

The Tainted Tormented Triangle Text (11/1/20 2:36p.m)

His Ex: Why are you ignoring me? I hate when you leave me on read,

Him: You need to relax, I already told you that our relationship is dead.

His Ex: You keep slandering me on social media, stop with your disrespect,

Him: I haven't said anything about you on the gram, trolls will be trolls, what do you expect?

His Ex: But you entertain it all the time; it's not cool, please stop it,

Him: You're still holding on to the past, just drop it.

His Ex: How dare you tell me I'm still holding on, I've been done, enough with the games,

Him: You keep calling me, just looking for some quick fame,

His Ex: I'm not looking for shit with you, just stop putting slander on my name.

Him: Whatever; stop with the DMs, stop calling my phone,

His Ex: Not until you give me your word that you will keep my name out your mouth, and you'll leave me alone.

Him: That's not me, tell that to the trolls, that's your problem not mine,

His Ex: Oh, so it's my problem now? Okay no problem, that's fine.

His Girl: Hey bae; I called you earlier, you didn't answer, you okay?

Him: Hey babe, nah not really, having a dramatic day.

His Girl: Aww, what happened? Is business going bad?

Him: No, it's my ex; she's losing it, this time she's gone mad.

His Girl: She's still in contact with you? By now she should be blocked,

Him: You're right; but she always manages to find a way on social media, it's like I'm stuck in this gridlock.

His Girl: Why don't you give me her number, we need to have a chat,

Him: No, let's not take that route, you don't have to do that.

His Girl: Oh yes we do, otherwise she's not going to stop this,

Him: Alright whatever; but just talk to her, afterwards I want to be done with this; dismissed.

His Girl: This is Samantha; I think we need to talk, are you free?

His Ex: "..."

Him: Hey babe; actually, don't bother, this has nothing to do with you, let it be.

His Girl: Baby, I'm not going to let her destroy our relationship,

Him: Babe, she's extremely thirsty, she'll do anything for a sip.

His Girl: I already sent her a message, she's typing, I see the three dots,

Him: Well whatever she says, just leave it on read, I want this madness to stop.

His Girl: Okay, but just block her from everything, she needs to understand that I'm going to be your wife,

Him: No doubt babe; you already know you're the love of my life.

His Girl: "Loved his message," Love you.

His Ex: Hey girl, I'm so glad you reached out,

We have so much that we need to talk about.

Let me just say that you're so sweet and so naive,

He can tell you anything and you'll so easily believe.

Did he tell you about that night when he missed your call,

How about the day you text him about your miscarriage, and he didn't respond at all?

Where do you think he was,

He was with me, doing what he does.

His Girl: You're full of shit, he wouldn't go back to you,

His Ex: There you go being naive again, damn you are such a fool.

His Girl: You would say anything just to break us apart,

His Ex: Well, here's a pic of us from last week, I'm sorry if this breaks your heart.

His Girl: Wow, well hey, maybe you both deserve each other,

His Ex: It's okay hunny, it happens to the best of us, you were just another,

His Girl: It's cool, because two can play at that game, I've been sleeping with his brother.

His Ex: Yes girl, spill that tea,

His Girl: Yep, so I think we have nothing more to talk about, unless there's something else you want to say to me?

His Ex: Nope, just that you're so sweet, yet so naive,

His Girl: Whatever, I'll take me leave.

His Ex: Just wanted you to know that your girl's a ho, a screenshot receipt,

Him: Whoa; you know you're messed up for this, this is low and weak.

His Ex: Go handle your business, I told you, you'll never find another like me,

Him: Let this be the last time we talk; don't call, text or DM; you're dead to me.

His Ex: "Loved his Message."

Him: So, we got some answers that we needed today,

His Girl: We sure did, is there anything that you want to say?

Him: Oh please, ladies first, I'm in no rush,

His Girl: I finally know why you weren't answering all those times, and why you were so hush, hush.

Him: I don't know what you're talking about hun,

His Girl: Oh, well here's a pic of you and her, out partying, having a lot of fun.

Him: Oh my God; are you serious?

His Girl: Yes, I'm serious, I'm hurt, and I'm fucking furious.

Him: This pic is from three years ago, before you and I ever met; she played you,

His Girl: Read at 3:22,

Him: Wow; and I never cheated on you,

His New Ex: Read at 5:02.

Him: You've been sleeping with my brother? I hope it was worth it, because I'm done with him and you.

"I faced birth as nothing,

I must face death as nothing.

Life in between is what I shall make of

it. "

Death (11/6/20 1:32 p.m.)

Death mentally text me every day, I always leave her on read,

She hates when I ignore her, she tries to seduce me in bed,

She wants to die like Shakespeare, she wants me dead.

I say hell no, now is not my time,

I'm not ready to go to eternal sleep, I'm doing just fine.

Death is such a groupie, she wants to meet everyone,

Old, young, human, animal; death, you're no fun.

I'm tired of the fear you put in my heart,

Blocked my conscious mind from growing smart.

You take when you're not welcomed, so not fair,

Do you have any remorse, regret, do you even care?

You better not take my children before you take me, don't

you dare.

I know you're going to have me, one way or another,

I'm trying to live the cleanest life I can, I have to declutter.

I wish I could live forever; I don't want you part of my life,

Forgive my selfishness, what do you have planned for me;

bullets, a disease, or how about a knife?

Sleep is the silent examination of our bodies,

Letting death know whose going, who's ready?

Funerals are the expensive apologies of death,

Looking down at the casket, enemies mentally celebrating

your last breath.

Life's a beautiful bitch, perhaps death is a jealous guy,

Perhaps death doesn't want us to enjoy life, it just wants us to roll over and die.

Maybe death is nothing more but a finish line to eternal rest,

Life is a reminder to live every day, a survivor's ultimate test,

Enjoy the journey, live for the moments, fulfill the quest.

Death; I am not a fan, yet I am not an enemy,

But before I have to knock on death's door, I ask you, the reader; please, please remember me.

The Gangster Who Forgave (11/2/20 10:04 p.m.)

A youngin came with a left hook, gangster falls to the
ground,
The youngin was showing off for his friends, not
understanding the gangster has been around.
The youngin had a gift, a preacher of wise words,
Not knowing the gangster is about that life, he shot people as
if they were birds.
The gangster got up, went around the corner,
Got his lemon, ready to squeeze, someone call the coroner.
The youngin was still there, turned up with his friends,
A car pulls up, tinted windows, all black Benz.
The gangster comes out of the car, the youngin is the main
target,
The youngin realized what he done is now his ultimate regret.
The gangster pressed the lemon to youngin's head,
Youngin's lemon drop tears begins to fall, he's as good as
dead.
Yet the gangster didn't squeeze the lemon, he put the lemon
away,
Youngin realizes that he's going to live, to see another day.
The gangster said, "You thought you were cool in front of
your friends, but where they go?

I could have ended your life, guaranteed at your funeral, half of them wouldn't even show."

Youngin said, "I apologize man, that was a stupid mistake,"

Gangster responded, "Not too many gangsters forgive, but your life, I'll spare to take."

Youngin understands the hard lesson learned, the gangster heads back into his car,

But before the gangster left, he said to youngin, "stay off these streets, focus on them books, let that knowledge take you far."

Interlude

My Dreams, My Truth

So, how are you feeling about this book so far? Are you enjoying it? Can you relate to anything you have read up to this point? Well, whatever you are feeling, I hope you are entertained in the process of reading these poems. But for right now, I would like to speak on some things that I have been holding on to for quite some time now.

I would like to talk about my dreams and the truth behind pursuing my dreams. I will elaborate as best as I can, to help you understand where I am coming from within this interlude. So, my dreams; it has been a dream of mine, to be a successful working actor. Since the age of eighteen, I have been training, studying, and pursuing an acting career. When I first caught the acting bug during my college years at

Centenary University, I never stopped moving forward. I kept going, kept achieving, and stayed focused. As of today, I am successful. I did make it to the union, which is "Screen Actors Guild-American Federation of Television Radio Artists." I have made it that far. I am proud of that achievement; however, I still have a ways to go. I have been in the union for over four years now, so far I cannot complain about my position in the business. Met a lot of amazing people; some I have kept in touch with over the years, and then there are those individuals who I hope I do not see, ever again.

I am sure you are thinking to yourself, "what is my point with all of this annotation?" Well, I told you my dream, but now I must share with you my truth. The truth, my truth; I have sacrificed having a normal life. Now, what do I mean by a "normal life?" Well, I have been so committed to my dreams, that I completely isolated myself from things that any young person would be doing in their twenties and thirties. I missed out on a lot of parties, the club life, dating, and just overall missing out on friendships.

For the last decade, I really did not focus on having that many realationships with people. Most of the friends I had, worked nine to five occupations. In show business, I could be on set from anywhere between twelve to fourteen hours a day, or longer. I never took the time to stop and think about making time for dating and just living my life. I did not put the dating life as a priority. I had some interest from time to time, as I mentioned earlier, but those interest were short lived, on both my side and the woman's side.

I realized that it was rather difficult to relate to a woman who works a nine to five job, who pretty much has settled with her life, and has her career in corporate America. It was difficult, telling her about all the exciting things I am doing on set, the different people I am meeting, all the ideas and plans I have, and other things that I had going on. Most of the women I met, they would say to me, "oh that's nice, well good luck." You know, one of those generic responses.

I guess it is hard for someone to relate to your dreams, especially if they do not have dreams of their own, or not pursuing their dreams. But when it comes to my dreams, the truth is, my dreams have left me in this state of loneliness that I talked about. I put so much time into pursuing my dreams, that I showed no dedication in maintaining a stabled balance with friends, family, and potential relationships. I became selfish; I went through a heavy selfish phase that has cost me dearly.

I cannot say that I have many friends, as of today. My phone does not receive many calls these days. Why is that?

Because people have forgotten about me. Oh, need I mention that I am no longer on social media. My first book, *"Logged Off: My Journey of Escaping the Social Media World,"* it tells you exactly why I had to remove myself from those platforms. I have been off of social media since the year 2018, and I have no plans on returning to those machines. If you ever read my first book, you will understand why I logged off.

But now, I have acknowledged the reality of my permanent isolation. I have paid a tremendous price by pursuing an acting career, by removing myself from social media, and by staying committed to my dreams. I literally avoided everyone, who I should say some were not supporters of mine. I was never into ass kissing for friendships or a relationship. As I said, I became selfish. I made time for friends, of course, when I had the time. But it was difficult at times when I was on set all day long. I cannot imagine being an actor and being a parent.

But I cannot tell you how many times after coming home, late at night, and not having anyone to talk to. That hurt at times, to be honest. Friendships that faded out, people who I once connected with, have now moved on, went their separate ways, and lost touch with them. All the hard work has paid off for me, it truly did. But now, with the price I

68

paid, I began to contemplate and ask myself, "was it all worth it?" Was chasing my dreams worth all the isolation? Am I happy with the result? As I was achieving my goals, yes there was happiness. However, I learned something about dreams.

Dreams are only dreams. They are not your life. We dedicate our lives to pursue our dreams. But our dreams cannot be our whole lives. It is unhealthy, rather a waste of life, to only focus on a dream, and not have a stabled balance of a social life, and when I mean social life, I am referring to real friends, people who you actually speak with in person. Not exactly the people you may share brief messages with on social media, or a random stranger you may never see in life.

That is what I learned about dreams. I share that with you, the reader; do not make dreams your whole life. It is very important that you have friends who love you for who you are, and that you have a great relationship with them. Friends who give you a call, just to reach out and possibly hangout with. That is very important and healthy.

There is that saying, "*be careful what you wish for.*" Boy is that so true; although now, I understand more of what that means. In my point of view, what it says to me is when I wish for something, the universe is asking, "is that all you wish for?" I understand now that when I speak it into the universe, whatever it is that I want in life, I have to be specific. I never asked the universe for friends, for a girlfriend or wife. All I wanted was to be a success. But hey, look what happened, I became a success, I have pursued my dreams, I am winning, and you are now reading my fourth book. The universe has responded to me. But to tell you the truth, what I did not ask the universe for, has not arrived in my life. I never spoke it into the universe to have a beautiful women, by my side, who also has dreams. I guess now I have to be very patient, not just with friendships and relationships, but also with my dreams. We have to be patient with life, period.

Do you understand what I have said in these several pages? Can you relate to me in any way, or am I alone on this one too? My overall point with all of this is I do not want you to put a blind eye to your needs, just so you could get everything that you want. I have had some rough nights, nights where I had to sleep on the loneliness. Nights where I felt I had no friends, no one to talk to, it felt like I did not even have dreams anymore. At least not the dreams worth holding on to.

Keep in mind, show business, the film industry, it is the most difficult game to break into. I am fortunate to even be in the actor's union. It is a crazy grind for sure. I gave up a lot in order to get what I want. The sacrifices, all the time and money invested into this business. You see, I do not have it all figured out, this thing we call life. I do not have all the answers, I hurt just like anyone else. Even if you may have a lot of money. What is the point of having millions, billions, if you have no one to share that wealth with? No real friends, no real love. We all have seen those millionaires who took their own lives, for whatever reason. But I am sure part of their reason was because they felt alone. Those poor people probably worked so hard their entire lives, dedicated their whole lives for a dream, and yes, the dream took them far, but what the universe will never tell you is dreams will take you farther and farther away from the people you love.

Your dreams will take you away from those who have your best interest at heart and surround you with the people who mean you harm. Now I must say, I am not a victim, nor do I paint the picture of being a victim. All I am saying is this, do not let your dreams get in the way of your blessings. Now what do I mean by that? What I mean is if there is ever a time when in your mind, your mind is telling you to take a break and enjoy life. Make sure you take that break and go out there and enjoy your life. Do not put yourself in overdrive, isolating yourself, killing yourself trying to pursue a dream.

Dreams eventually fade out and become opaque. Sometimes if you are pursuing a dream for so long, the dream weakens your sight, and you can no longer see it, you cannot see anything clearly anymore, and then you eventually lose sight of it. But it is always a good friend or a mentor, who comes along and gives you some encouragement, a new dream even, where you have a clear vision. Just like with writing. I did not see myself becoming a published author, that was a dream I never saw coming. I did not see that vision, until the universe put those new ideas in my mind, gave me that new vision, and I saw it through.

I guess every so often, we have to change our dreams, and by changing our dreams, we automatically change our circle of friends. Perhaps that is what has happened in my life right now. I am in the process of a different dream, another destiny so to speak, and within it, I am in this lonely stage.

That is the thing about life; you just never know what it will present to you. It comes with good surprises and bad surprises. We all want more of the good ones than the bad, but we just never know. But if I may, let me also say this to you, the reader. If by any chance, what you have read just now, if this relates to you, or you can reflect, I want you to know, that you are not alone.

Again, I do not have all the answers, I do not know everything. But if you got anything out of what I said right here, I say be careful with your dreams. Dreams do not make you. Only you can make the dreams come true. But do not over pursue, do not overly prioritize your dreams to the point where you have lost yourself and others, simply because you are trying to make your dreams come true.

Do you know why people are excited when their dreams come true? It is because there is some type of reward, a trophy, a prize that awaits the winner. We work so hard for a prize, a trophy, or a ring. But we miss out on other things that are of much more value and importance. The great late John Lennon said it best, in his own way, *Life is what happens to you, while you're busy making other plans.*" Let me tell you, I spent a lot of years ignoring life, while I was making those other plans, and I most definitely paid for that.

But I have no regrets that I live with. I have had regrets, of course, but by no means do I live with those regrets. As I live, I continue to learn. I learn more and more about myself, and now I am less of a planner, and more of a person who lives. I just let life take its' course, I keep moving forward, and I appreciate just being alive.

Yes, it would be lovely if I had a more stabled circle of friends, it would be great to have that support system of a girlfriend by my side, but again, I must be patient. I also must know that when I meet that special one, that it is up to me to make that happen, to make that move. I do not know when that will be. Again, life is filled with random surprises. But in the meantime, I must continue to live, and as long as I have my true friend, which is tomorrow, I will be alright.

I know I may be alone on this one, many of you readers may not relate to what I am saying, or maybe some of you are. My loneliness is not a product of desperation. It is a product of being unbalance with life. For the past twelve years, I have lived a very one-sided lifestyle. A lifestyle that was all about my dreams. I would say seventy-five percent of my life was dedicated to my dreams, and only the remaining twenty-five percent went to any form of a social life.

I think when people have success, fortune, and fame, then people will be drawn to them. But that is not always the healthiest way to attract people, the people with good intentions I should say.

To be honest with you, life is a dream. When we put a dream within a dream, we violate the preordained blessings we already have coming to us. Think about those people who played the lottery only a handful of times, maybe even one time, and they hit the jackpot for millions of dollars. But for some people, they are devoted to playing the lottery every

74

single day, but never really win. I do believe that there are things that are in our control and there are things that we have no control over. You are in control of what dreams you choose to pursue in your life, but you are not in control of where those dreams may take you. I never knew my dreams of being a working actor would lead me down a road of becoming a published author.

But anyways, that was just some rambling I wanted to get off of my chest. This is not about friends, or dating, this was about choices. Choose wisely how you live your life. Have balance with your life, do not over pursue your dreams and not live. Use your dreams as a tool, not as a way of life. Dreams are just a rat race with a finish line, and not everyone who crosses the finish line will win first place or win a prize.

When you think about it, being born is really a dream come true. Being born is winning first place. The fact that you outswam a colossal amount of sperm cells to the finish line of being conceived. Being born is the only dream none of us asked for. We were just blessed with it. I understand now that you really have to just give life a break. You were born, that is a gift in itself, the ultimate gift. What more could you possibly want?

As I said, life is a dream that is meant to be lived, and not to be confused about. There really are no secrets to life, no answers really. There are lessons to be learned, wisdom to be gained, and knowledge to be protected.

This is my truth; I pursued my dreams in an unhealthy way. With no balance, not many friends, not so many life memories. But I am still young, not that tomorrow is promised to any of us, but now I look forward to remedying my dedication, and try my best to live life with enjoyment rather than torment. Do not ever do what I did; do not torment yourself, do not lie to yourself, believing that you do not need anybody, you do not need friends or family to support you. Yes, it is possible to live without having a spouse, but we all want to be loved and appreciated.

I thought that prize at the end of the finish line was worth the smiles, but the smiles were only for the pictures. When I came home with the trophy, I came home with tears of loneliness. No phone calls from friends saying congratulations, unless if I posted it on social media, which again, I am no longer active on.

But yea, those were my dreams and my truth. Perhaps it is not all about me. Maybe one of my purposes in life is to inspire someone who I have never met, and probably will never meet. Inspire them to have a dream that they bring into reality. They speak it into existence and work hard to achieve it the right way. With patience and integrity, and I wish you well.

That is all I have to say about that. Something to think about when it comes to dreams. For now, let us continue with "*A Lonely Rose.*"

"God gives missions and quests; the Devil gives jobs and orders."

Sex Was Not Invited   (11/13/20 12:28 p.m.)

I cried at her beauty, is she real?

Her body is of immaculate perception, I consensually touch, I feel.

I feel her body, her softness, her lotion scented skin,

I feel her pulse, her vibration, her life force within.

Hair all the way down to her back, silky and smooth,

My hands become lost in the caressing of her hair; it's real, let it sooth.

She dismissed the clothes from her body, naked in the nature of my sight,

I stare with worshiping interest; I'm bleeding of pleading for her to stay the night.

She blessed me with a growing yes,

I begin to join her in nude as I undress.

Two naked beings, we stare, we gazed,

We love what we see, we're in sync, amazed.

Would you find it strange that we didn't invite sex to this party; hope sex doesn't mind,

I just want to appreciate her body, let the vision of her marinate in my mind.

We explored our presence, without the distraction of intercourse,

An absence of fornication, nothing forced.

We embraced our scents, our energy, an experience
worthwhile,
She appreciated my respect for her body, her chastity, she
gave me the perfect smile.
We both invited our clothes back on, a naked secret we kept,
Cuddled with appreciation, in each other's arms we slept,
She had to ignore the "D," as it began to erect,
We watched the news on ABC, then "Z's" we began to
collect,
Sex is not an answer, but the reward for coming correct.

Fear   (11/6/20 11:33 a.m.)

Free us from the penitentiary gates,

Streets filled with demons, repent before it's too late.

Praying to God with fear in the heart,

Doubt in the brain, is death the end or an eternal start?

Why do we have to believe instead of knowing,

Panic in the streets keeps growing and growing.

How do they expect us to stay sane,

While Sept 11th is still replaying in our brains?

The curse of disease still breathes,

Viruses in our iris and sinuses, they're thieves,

What do you fear? Tell me please.

"Social media can make you overestimate your value and importance to other people's lives."

The Man with No Name (11/2/20 10:16 p.m.)

She lays tiresome on the soft comfy couch, watching her
favorite show,

Lights are off, kids are asleep, her face has that tv glow.

She goes up to check on the kids, but they are not in bed,

On the bed there was a note that said, "tonight miss
babysitter, you'll be dead."

Her heart began to sink to the floor,

Then came a slam; it was the slamming of a door.

Terror and fear running through her veins,

Anxiety and paranoia dancing in her brain.

She called for the kids, yet all she received were the echoes
of her voice bouncing off the walls,

Slowly walking with caution, in the dark and eerie hall.

Another note on the floor, she picks it up and reads,

It said, "turn around," when she did, she ran at full speed.

A supernatural presence, she ran to the bathroom and locked
the door,

Fear rises as she hears footsteps creaking the wooden floor.

Knock, knock; she's afraid to ask who's there,

A knock again, but her brain says, "don't you dare."

Then a harder knock is given, she begins to scream,

A complete breakdown, it's like she's in a bad dream.

A final knock, this time, a child's voice she hears,

She runs to unlock the door, it was the kids, presented with
fear and tears.

She asked, "where were you guys? You had me scared to
death,"

One said, "We hide from him, he came after our parents left."

The babysitter asked, "Who? Who came?"

They said, "The man, the man with no name."

Another door unlocks, the parents have returned from a
lovely evening,

The babysitter comes down with the kids, parents asked,
"why aren't they sleeping?"

The babysitter responded, "You put them to bed, I'm
leaving."

The father runs after her, while the mother stands by her
daughter and son,

The proud mother kneeled down to her kids and said, "I knew
the prank would work, I knew she would run."

The mother then takes the kids back up the stairs,

Smiling with revenge after catching her husband and the
babysitter having an affair.

Husband came back inside and said, "Well, she's not coming
back, that's for sure,"

The wife responded, "Yea, I hope you said goodbye to your
filthy little whore."

I Come From   (11/14/20 12:00 a.m.)

A city of Crips and Bloods, R.I.P. and graves dug,

Who's your plug, you a thug, fiends begging for drugs.

Not a land of dreams coming true,

What set you banging, red or blue?

Gentrified your block, Jews buy the property,

Coming in like one-eyed Willy, pirates taking over like a
monopoly.

Kids were once running in playgrounds, now they're running
for their lives,

Demons in the streets, whispering the Devil's lies,

Mommies and daddies burying their babies, the screams and
cries.

More caskets getting wet than baskets hitting nothing but net,

Judges throwing the book at youngins who can't even read,

Uneducated minds behind bars, incarcerated seeds.

Who cares for boys and girls with the kinky hair,

Coming from an environment where you can catch a bullet,
over a five second stare.

Is blackness a curse,

Can't change who you are, no matter how many times you
rehearse.

I come from the hood,

Where there's more concrete than grass and wood,

Where there's homies, the phony, and bad boys up to no
good.

Gunshots now, flowers later;

I give you this message now but save it for later.

The more divided we are, the greater we become,

But the more united we are, the more haters were among.

I come from the hood,

Where do you come from? I hope someplace good.

My complexion is not bulletproof, I too need protection,

Hard to survive in an atmosphere of gunshots and sirens,
bullet wounded infections.

How do you call a place your home,

When you have a Glock pressed against your dome?

They want to send you to Jesus quick,

Lemon squeezing, empty clips,

They pulled a John Lennon on Nip,

Red for the Bloods, white for the Clan, and blue for the
Crips?

Open your mind and let it marinate on that,

Tears engraved on the skin within, in loving memory tatts.

I come from, damn.

Celebrity Curse   (11/14/20 10:41 p.m.)

Millions in the bank, fronting on the gram,

Uninvited intruders rob the house, I'll be God damn.

Cameras and paparazzi, nowhere to hide,

Anxiety and fear captured at every angle, paranoia growing

swiftly inside.

News feeds spreading rumors, begging the media to stop,

Rappers drop, heartbeats stop, what happened to hip hop?

Money buys the diamond watches and rings,

But you can't take it with you, so money isn't everything.

Interviews, questions, tell me about yourself,

Interrogations, no therapist for the mental health.

Fame is the fugazi flame that fans keep fanning to increase

the flames,

Popular names mixed with political games for political gain,

Political parties; not invited, the guest list removed their

names.

They got played; they were used, abused, and refused,

The political games are over, now they're meme food.

Attention is the new currency, they want the masses to pay

attention,

Too poor to pay attention, COVID has us on face mask

detention,

Checks bouncing, bills piling, credit card suspension.

No money from tours, the virus has global expansion,

Celebrities going insane in their multi-million-dollar mansions?

Interviewers asking old questions, but the people don't care,

Same ole questions grow old like the celebs, minus the gray hair.

Laughter; feeling sorry for the rich more than the poor,

Idols becoming idle, Only Fans make them go viral,

A generation of babies heading towards a downward spiral.

Some pray to Jesus while others prays due to Allah,

Expecting miracles to end racism like TADAH,

Dismiss calling each other black and white and you'll get your "Uh-Hah."

Celebrities; oh my, you have been blessed, but it came with curses,

At war with each other, enslaved to the Birkin bag purses,

People are still dying, coughing on their nurses,

Worrying about how many followers they have when 99% of them won't be following behind their hearses.

Go your own way people, stop looking for a savior or leader,

All you need is education; be wise, be an avid reader.

The choice is always and truly yours,

Again, don't feel sorry for the rich more than the poor.

Scandal They Couldn't Handle (11/17/20 1:26 p.m.)

Money on his mind, so she kissed his frontal lobe,

Steamy seductive figure blanketed in her bathrobe.

The lack of his knowledge, unaware of her unfaithful

pleasures,

He thinks he's found gold, the rarest of treasures.

But what he found was true heartache, her cheating game has

no rules,

She plays the men, plays them for fools.

No shame in her game, she's a master of disaster,

He couldn't cheat if he dared, can't put nothing past her.

She has men holding on to her like an umbrella in a storm,

When she's ready to quit them, a pretty demon is born.

She takes their gifts; bags, diamonds, and shoes,

Men tell her, "anything you want baby, anything you choose."

She wants the most expensive, burning holes in men's

pockets,

But they can't escape her, overly addicted to her vaginal

socket.

Her body is to die for,

Her truth is to lie for,

Her absence is to cry for,

Her die is to ride for.

But these men have yet learned,

When you play with fire, expect to be burned.

She was the fire they could never put out,

She could have any man she wants; facts, without a doubt.

Is she wrong for her confidence without commitment,

Taking from these men; no remorse or resentment?

Perhaps women only live, and men only learn,

Men wasting their time waiting in line, begging for a turn.

She has these men waiting on her hands like feminine nails,

Once she gets salty on them, they began to disappear, like snails.

She can kiss a man's soul out of his flesh,

A Kodak moment when she's dressed in Fashion Nova mesh.

For every man she has a scandalous plan,

Men treat her like a superstar, and she treats them like a fan.

She's out there, men beware,

She's poppin; long hair, don't care,

Don't be a fool, pursue if you dare,

Men are her toys, and she doesn't share,

Keep playing her game, knowing she doesn't play fair.

A Venting Rose (11/18/20 7:02 p.m.)

Hello again, I thought I would give you a break from the poetry for now. I hope you are enjoying them so far. We still have a long journey ahead of us, but I wanted to give you a breather for a moment. I am sure that by now you have realized that my work is rather unbiased. It does not cater to one specific group of people. My work is for all people. I feel that is the best way to connect with people, by writing something that everyone can relate to. People of all different ethnicities, different nationalities, people from all different walks of life.

That is what makes me feel completely free when I write. When it comes to my books, I want for every and anyone who picks up a copy of my work, as they begin reading, they find themselves in the stories. Perhaps something that actually happened to them in their lives. I want you as the reader, to be able to see a reflection of yourself. To let you know that you are not invisible and that you are not alone. Your presence in the world is not only seen but appreciated. That is what I want you to feel when you open up my books.

I thought this would be a good time to take a rest from the poems, and to do some venting, as I did in my last book, *"The Healing."* Earlier I talked about my dreams and my truth. To be honest with you, I am now at peace with myself, more than I have ever been. I am at peace because I was able to let go and release that acknowledgement of self, that I have been hiding within myself for so many years. I really felt that I committed so much time out of my life to my dreams, that I really ignored living the real dream, which is life.

Life truly is a dream, it can be a very stressful, heartbreaking dream from time to time, but it can also be oh so beautiful. I believe the world is an extremely beautiful creation, if only more people would see and respect it in that way. I see beauty in the world much more now since my permanent departure from the social media world. But yes, reality is too real at times. We always receive our wake-up calls when we least expect them.

You know, as I have been writing for the whole year of 2020, I learned something about myself that I have to remove from my way of living. I really spend way too much time thinking of my past, what I could have done better, and how I try to prevent it from happening in the future. I also think about the future too much as well. I had to work on living in the moment. But what I did not understand before, I sincerely understand now. I understand that to really live in the moment, it is better to share most of those moments with people you truly care about, and who truly cares about you. To live in the moment with someone else, it is a better memory to hold onto.

I feel that I did not create enough of those moments in my twenties. I was more focused on the moments of being on set, posting selfies on social media, and simply living a selfish lifestyle. I must admit, I just could not beg anyone for a friendship, I could not beg anyone to reach out to me, to see how I was doing. I understand that life is life and we all have to go our own way in the real world. But I do not know, maybe I was too anti-social for people's liking.

I am not much of a talker, but I am working on being more social. Well, I actually do talk with people, and I have great conversations, but my absence on social media has limit my connection with people. If you have not read my first book, "Logged Off," I had to make a choice, I had to escape those platforms. Truth be told, I felt the loneliest when I used social media than what I felt after I logged off.

My God, I learned so much about myself after I left, yet I still have so much to learn about life, about who I can trust, what do I believe in, or where do I see myself five years from now? Ten years from now? There I go again, thinking about the future. You see? I am still a work in progress. I should only speak for myself, but I am sure many out there may feel the same, as far as being a work in progress.

How do you feel? I mean, obviously I won't know your response to this question, but ask yourself, how do you feel? I am sure you are thinking in your mind right now and you are saying, "how do I feel about what?" How do you feel about the life you are living at this moment? How do you feel about yourself? Is there balance in your life? Is there someone you want to have in your life, but are not able to have them? Is there a loved one who has passed away that you would love to talk to again? Maybe for some people, they do not possess these feelings at all.

Some people tuck their true feelings deep inside their conscious, never to release them. Some people do not know how to properly express themselves, which is why they always express themselves through anger. I never was an angry guy, never really had hatred for another person. But I have dealt with individuals, who I would say have put me to the test, and I said this before, misery and pain welcomes company. There are a lot of hurt people out there, a lot of people who are a lonely rose, floating away to an unknown destiny.

Let me tell you something, I believe there are no answers in life, there are only the results of the choices that we make in our lives. I spent so many years of my life, looking for answers, trying to change my past. But how I could I possibly change the past? I simply cannot. We can really create misery for ourselves when we try to find answers to fill in the blanks to what happened in the past. Now, do not get me wrong; if it is a situation such as a murder investigation, by all means, solve that crime. But what I am really referring to is when we go through life's challenges, we give it our absolute best, and even then, we may not achieve our goals, or our dreams, and what I hope you would avoid, is dedicating years of your life, looking for answers to why you came up short and failed.

Failure can eat you alive and leave not a trace. Believe me, I have failed at some things in life. I failed friendships, relationships with women, failed test and classes, I have had a fair share of failures in my life. But what I believe my worst failure is, was looking at my past and trying to decorate it with answers, trying to make it look more appealing, even if it is only for myself.

Do you understand me? Have I made sense to you? What I am basically saying to you, the reader, is that I was simply burying my misery, my pain, and my failure, with bullshit answers, thinking that I was going to forget my past, or that I could possibly run away from it. Until I finally understood that my past is, and will always be a part of who I am. Whether it was good, bad, ugly, maybe a little evil at times. It is still a part of me. There are things in my past that I am not proud of, but not too many. But I am proud of the fact that I did not let those disappointing moments from my past defeat me. I am very proud of the man that I have become. As I live in the moment, I live with pride. I know my worth more than ever now. My self-worth; I may not mean much to the world, the world does not even know that I exist. Which is why life is truly whatever you make of it. As long as you bring more joy in this world than misery.

That is a funny feeling; the fact that you, myself; the world may not even know you and I even exist. We are just these two human beings, living on this planet at this very moment, we are existing, but to the world, we do not exist. Unless if you are a celebrity, or a world-famous billionaire. That is why I feel at times, like a lonely rose. I mean here I am, this is my fourth book, and I have no idea who will read my work. Chances are you the reader, I may never see you in this life. But you are reading my work. You are at this very moment, reading what I wrote. You took a chance, you made a choice in reading my book, even though we may never meet or see each other in this lifetime. I just find that to be so strange, yet so magical and appreciative. I appreciate you for taking the time out of your life to read my work, to give it a chance. It lets me know that you too exist on this earth. If you please, do me a favor. If you ever were to see or meet me in this life, and you read this book, make sure you say this to me, "*Two lonely roses existing in the same garden.*" What I mean by that is the two of us have met in this garden we call the earth, and we both acknowledge our existence on the very same earth. That would actually mean a lot to me.

But then again, it is not all about me. Maybe one of my purposes in life is to inspire someone who I have never met, and probably will never meet. Inspire them to have a dream that they bring into reality. To speak it into existence and work hard to achieve it the right way. With patience and integrity. If that is one of my purposes in life, I wish that person the very best.

But anyways, these are my thoughts, my ideas, and my opinions. What do you think? I mean, we are just these human beings, on this one tiny little pebble we call the planet earth, floating and orbiting in a colossal space. We have holidays, paydays, birthdays, and death dates. We have all these checkpoints of moments in our lives, so many memories to be captured. As I said, there are really no answers in life, but just the results of the choices we make.

When you look at the world, we see all the bad things and ask ourselves, "what are the answers?" Well, the answer to that question is there are no answers. What you choose to do or not do is all the power you truly have in this life. Some people choose to do bad things. But to be fair, not everyone chooses to have bad things happen to them. The victimization in this world is real, but I believe that our society has made being a victim popular. You can easily become a superhero or celebrity by being a victim. I feel that energy sends off a crippling message to the youth.

Because what ends up happening is this; real victims will try to convince themselves that what they went through does not require any professional help. The real victims will try to bury their pain with success. That is why social media has become more of a curse than a gift. You see more people on social media crying for help while their likes and followers are increasing. However, the pressure that comes with being a superhero in today's world, there is no one whose shoulder the hero can cry on in the time of need. No one ever prays for the hero. Well, maybe I should not say no one prays, some do. Heroes can become lonely as well.

But yea, with this book specifically, this was not a book meant for you as the reader to be over thinking. I did not want you to feel that you had to do a lot of brainstorming to understand this book. Now of course, I was not going to make this a bland piece of writing. But I just wanted you to be more relaxed and make you feel; feel the words, feel essence within the pages. I did not want it to be this controversial, politically charged piece of writing. I truly wanted you to know that even though you may feel lonely at times in your life; I want you to know that you are not alone. Your existence on this earth may not be a famous one, but your existence matters tremendously. Society may try to convince you otherwise, but again, life is whatever you make it to be.

I thought about this philosophy, and now I live by this. I said, "*I faced birth as nothing, I must face death as nothing, and life in between is what I make of it.*" I look at birth and death as parenthesis, the life that is in between is all that truly counts. Better yet, I look at birth and death more like quotations marks. Perhaps that gives life in between, a much more enthusiastic meaning. Our birth and our death are none of our business; we have no control over them. None of us asked to be born, nor do we have a choice of dying. Life is our only business.

That is why I try my absolute best to avoid phony people, consistent liars, and simply go my own way. To make this life meaningful to me, and not for the fulfillment of the fantasies that are expected of me, by other people.

So, when I said in the beginning of this book, about not feeling sorry for me, I truly mean that, sincerely. I am not a desperate man, I am in a good place, really. But I am still human, loneliness does come and go. However, I have found my outlet, and my outlet is what you are holding right now in your hands. My outlet is writing; all the pain, all the hurt, the loneliness, or whatever it is that I am feeling inside, I write it and I share it with you. I do not feel sorry for myself; I do not live in misery. I just accept those moments for what they are and move forward. I do not worry about friends not calling back. As far as I am concerned, the greatest friend I have in this life is tomorrow. As long as I have tomorrow, I have another chance to mold my life into a better piece of existence.

But anyways, that is all I had to say about that. A little venting so to speak. I actually feel so much better writing about how I feel, than it ever felt when I would post it on social media. When you write about what you feel, the paper does not judge you. The paper does not agree or disagree with you. It allows your pen to just bleed with no regrets. With that being said, let's go into the next poem, *"The End of 2020."*

The End of 2020   (11/19/20 9:52 p.m.)

Illegal purchases, rap battle verses,

Churches praying for the nurses,

Kids not going to God, they're going to Google searches.

Seek vengeance on social media,

Programming platters they're feeding ya.

Scary games, so many political names,

The virus killed the tours and fame,

This world may never be the same,

A crying shame but not enough tears for wildfire flames,

Ironic how it's so far away from hurricanes.

Video games sold all the way out; no more Xbox and PS5,

Every year we bite a new Apple, technology to keep the addiction alive,

Everyone's home; babysitting while working their nine to five.

Economy took a commercial dive, the money can't swim,

Bubble NBA, no crowds or fans in the way, a win is a win?

A recount for votes; who's being honest, who's only kidding,

Take notes kids, the next election will have a lot information hidden.

People looking for vaccines,

More famous now than Michael Jackson,

More cases, more faces, different places, face mask on
during tax season.
We pray to God for help while he begged us to stop,
The second coming is here as the temperature begins to drop.
Coughing and sneezing, hospital beds filled with wheezing,
The Devil's so happy, he can't stop cheezing.
Live your life; you're too alive,
Your life matters; stand tall and thrive.
Not everything you see will be of sorrow or tragic,
Tomorrow is your greatest friend, tomorrow will bring you
the magic.
Two months away before we reach the finish line,
One of the most tragic years of all time.
Lost a G.O.A.T. and his baby girl,
Lost jobs and money; such a bankrupt world.
But we didn't lose hope; I hope?
I think I've seen it all when I saw Instagram invaded by the
Pope.
If you're reading this, you've made it to the year 2021, May
this year bring you nothing but peace, love, success, and
ultimate fun,
Okay, I think I'm done.

She Danced with The Devil (11/20/20 12:00 a.m.)

The house grew quiet, broken glass and dishes,

God, if she could go back in time, if she had three wishes.

Tears mixed with her blood and makeup,

She just survived an abusive breakup.

Hands were thrown her way, another fight she loses, Her

body covered with a black and blue dress of bruises. She's

unable to move, her body's crawling on the floor, The bell

rings, her neighbor is at the door.

An unlocked door, the neighbor sees her on the floor,

The neighbor tries to pick her up; but she screams, her body

is swollen and sore.

Her neighbor asked, "did your husband put hands on your

face?"

She responded, "yes, I don't know what happened, his mind

was in another place."

Her neighbor said, "you have to call the police, this is a

crime,"

She said, "oh no, this was the first time, I'll be fine."

Frustration poured through the neighbor's eyes,

How could this woman live with these abusive lies?

The neighbor said, "you're only lying to yourself, but it's

your life,"

She said, "he needs me, I'm...I'm his wife."

The neighbor said, "at least go to the hospital, you're in bad shape,"

With anger she responded, "just mind your business, just go home with your bullshit cape,"

The neighbor walked out the door, as the wife closed the tapestry drapes.

Morning comes, the neighbor hears police sirens, something's wrong,

The neighbor walked outside, it was like a scene out of a movie, minus the sad song.

The neighbor finds the first officer she sees, she asked, "is she, is she...dead?"

The officer pulled her to the side and hesitatingly said, "we, we can't find her head."

She lost it, heavily breathing, chills shooting up and down her spine,

She doesn't know what to say, think, or feel, she lost her mind.

She began to cooperate with the officers, gave them the husband's name,

She wanted to go home and minded her business, she felt the blame.

They said, "thank you for your cooperation, you can now go,"

She went back home, but she walked oh so slow.

The guilt, the trauma of seeing her, now knowing she's dead,

What's worst; officers are still searching for her head.

The neighbor; trying to rest in the middle of the night,

Her doorbell rings, twice, woke her up with a chilling fright,

She looked at her doorbell camera, but there was no one in sight.

Nothing there but a box; too late for a package delivery,

Traumatized by what happened, she moves toward her door with a knife and uncontrollable shivery.

The shaking of her hand gave the doorknob an earthquake as she turns it,

She opened the door, saw the box with a note that said, "You've earned it."

Very hesitant to open up the box, she leaves it outside,

She got nervous and called the cops, waited until they arrived.

The cop came; the box remained in front the neighbor's house,

A knock on her door, it was the cop, he came in as quiet as the breathing of a mouse.

She told the officer, "I didn't want to open the box, I didn't want to know what was inside,"

The officer brought it in, opened it, kaboom to his face; she screamed, but he died."

Out of nowhere, her neighbor's husband is standing at the front door,

He said, "I already have my wife's head, now I want yours."

She screamed throughout her house, chased by her neighbor's killer,

But it's not the end, prepare for part two of this thriller.

A Mother's Escape to Paradise (11/20/20 8:20 p.m.)

A hard-working mother, a mother of four,

She said, "I've had enough," as she stormed out and swiftly slammed the door.

She left her nagging husband, her children and pets,

She took a long drive, hotel reservations all set.

Her husband calls, yet she doesn't pick up the phone,

He then sent a text, pleading with her to come back home.

She drove down a lonely road, a road of pure azure and clear waters,

She begins her fallen tears as she starts to think about her son and three daughters.

Guilt in her consciousness, she can't believe what's she's done,

How does she leave her children, especially her ten-year-old son?

Her husband calls again, still she has no answer for him,

The stress of being a mother 24/7, has grown within.

She arrives at her hotel, not far from the breathtaking views of the beach,

The sun shining so peacefully, if the sun had a face, she'd kiss his cheek.

She made her way into her hotel room,

Plopped on the bed and did an hour of teary doom and gloom.

She cried herself to sleep, then woke up in total darkness,

She checked her phone, let there be light, she received a text from her son Marcus.

Marcus said, "hi mom, just wanted to say I love you, please come home,"

She responded, "I love you too," tear drops hitting the screen of her phone.

She walks into the bathroom, a deep stare at herself in the misty mirror,

Staring with disbelief, she wipes the glass to see herself clearer.

She looked and said to herself, "you coward; how could you leave your family alone?"

It's just not easy when her daughter's autism is set in stone.

When her husband is a sip away from 12-steps,

And her oldest daughter dancing for money, stripping off her fishnets.

A lot on her plate, too stressed to eat,

She takes a trip down to the pool, to sit and wet her feet.

As she sits alone, a voice comes from the other side of the pool,

It was a man's voice, he said, "I would love to join you, if it's cool?"

A lonely mother wouldn't turn down company of another,

A deep conversation they commit to; two wet feet now
became four,

They stare up at the moon, stars galore.

He asked where she is staying, she said, "I'm sorry, but I
have a husband,"

He responded, "oh I see, no problem, I understand."

She doesn't want him to go, she has a lot to get off her
shoulders,

He then looked in her eyes, kissed her cheek, and began to
hold her.

She told him her truth and asked for his,

He hesitated, then courageously said, "okay, here it is."

He had a truth for her that needed revealing,

He said to her, "if you can accept me as I am, you would be
giving me healing."

She asked, "what do mean? I don't understand."

He told her, "I have transitioned, from woman to man."

The makeup of shock quickly baked her face,

Swiftly she took a few steps away from him, she wanted
some space.

She said, "I don't believe you, I wouldn't have ever known,

He responded, "yea, believe it or not, this is me, a true
identity of my own."

The shock effect quickly fades, she becomes more open with
him,

She respects his identity and doesn't judge what he feels within.

He said to her, "thank you for still standing here with me,

Most of the time when I tell people, they disappear, they flee."

She responded, "I would never do that, you're...you're a great man,"

He gave her his handsome smile with a kiss, a gently kiss on her hand.

As he held her close, he said, "let us remember this night of Miami vice,"

She humorously responded, "yes, I'll remember it as the day I escaped and found paradise."

Lost at Sea   (11/25/20 1:54 p.m.)

A disconnect is in the making,

A family bond, gone for the taking.

A daughter uneducated, slaving away,

She's had enough, she must break free, she must get away.

Run away, run away, but where can she go,

This life is all she knows; they say to her, "if you leave,

you'll be declared foe."

Her brain screams "leave," but her heart cries for her parents,

She doesn't want them to look at her as a treason tyrant.

She went to her parents, gave them a piece of her awakened

mind,

She was shut down immediately, their support is what she did

not find.

She signed on the dotted affidavit line,

Walking away is the ultimate crime,

Trapped with these freeloaded fines.

Trapped in a mind-controlled cage,

Surrounded by policy breathing entities who are enraged,

So many books, yet no one's on the same page.

Yet she escaped; a parent-less daughter out on the run,

She feels reborn, gazing at the eternal sun,

She's lived a life of childhood labor, where was the fun?

Life goes on, twenty years is coming near,

She hasn't spoken to her parents since she escaped, their
demise is what she fears.

A miracle has appeared, a familiar face she once called her
mother,

She found her mother on Facebook, and she has a fifteen-
year-old baby brother.

It's been almost twenty years, what can she write, what will
she say,

She wrote a long message to her mother, pressed send; she
waits, she prays.

A notification rises, her heart begins to race,

She begins to read her mother's message; my God, if you
could only see her face.

She's overwhelmed with relief that her parents have escaped
as well,

Her mother said, "you were right to leave baby, you managed
to escape pure hell."

A tearful daughter begs to see her family ASAP,

Technology is a beautiful blessing; they saw each other
through the FaceTime app.

A burst of tears as they see each other through their screens,

Afraid they would never see each other again; it feels like
such a dream.

A deserted daughter says to her parents, "I'm so hurt that you
chose an abusing lie over your own kid,"

Her parents said, "forgiveness is what we beg of you, we are
so sorry for what we did."
"I forgive you," is what she peacefully said,
Her remorseful parents can finally put their guilt to bed.
The daughter said good night and booked a flight, she's going
to see her family,
In the air, she sees nothing but clear water ocean, as her
family lives in Miami.
She arrives; collected her bags, and she waits,
Thirty feet away, she sees her family, it's a miracle, it's fate.
She runs to her parents and brother, a family hug, oh so tight
and real,
More tears to refill the sea, this is the time to heal.
The hidden riddle of inherited insanity,
How does one dehumanize thousands in order to save
humanity?
A family once disconnected, lost at sea, reunited once again,
They pray that other families who are lost at sea, will see the
light once again,
And emancipate from this mentally enslaving machine, the
betrayal rape of mundane.

"I believe that the less labels we put on ourselves, the clearer we know who we truly are."

Pick Up the Phone (11/23/20 6:58 p.m.)

She calls, she waits, four rings then a voice mail,

She's sorry; sorry for the lies and disrespect, for putting him through hell.

Ten minutes goes by, she taps her screen to make another call,

But he doesn't answer, he doesn't answer at all.

Twenty text later she calls him once more,

Straight to voice mail she goes, she said, "baby please forgive me, I won't lie anymore."

Wiping her eyes while she's texting more lies,

Her battery's running low, better plug up before it dies.

She wants to call again, but her patience is drying up like her teary face,

Her heart's beating at a fast pace,

She didn't mean to hurt him; she just wanted her space.

She looked at her phone, ready to call,

Then it slipped out of her hands, took a face first fall.

She picked up her phone, a colossal crack left its mark,

A screensaver of them together, yet the crack in between set them apart.

A vibration to her phone, he gives her a call,

She apologized madly; his response took a stall.

She said, "I don't want to lose you, but a commitment is what I fear,"

He responded, "This is not good for me, tell me what I want to hear."

But she can't, like her phone, she leaves his heart with a crack,

Before he hung up, he said, "just lose my contact."

Late that night, she went to his diner workplace,

When she arrived, he had a blank look on his face.

She ran to him, into his arms, everyone watched, everyone stared,

She held him so tight, people kept looking, but she didn't care.

He said, "Please let's take this outside,"

She said, "When you hung up on me, I just broke down and cried,"

He responded, "But you don't want me, you said you did, but you lied."

A fragrance of frustrations gives her energy a stench,

They took a walk over to the bus station bench.

He said, "You still don't want a relationship, just tell me why,"

As she looked at him, she fixed her lips together and said, "I...I...I"

A Conversation Never Had   (11/25/20 8:11 p.m.)

African American Man: No if, and, or but about it, you're a racist man,

Caucasian Man: I'm not a racist, you assume I am, it's just when it comes to rap, I'm not a fan.

A.A.M: No, you are; if you deny it, you're lying,

CM: I tell you I'm not, if I'm lying, I'm flying.

A.A.M: So, what do you have to say about Black Lives Matter?

CM: I say it won't matter if blacks kill other blacks, it's hypocrisy for that matter.

A.A.M: Wait a minute; what are you trying to say about blacks killing blacks?

CM: Yea, what about black people killing themselves, what do you say to that?

A.A.M: Okay, but who put the guns and drugs in our communities?

CM: Not me; I have no power or responsibility for that, perhaps that's the government's impunity.

A.A.M: But I bet you've put a blind eye to racist acts, didn't you?

CM: Don't judge me okay, don't assume what I would or wouldn't do.

A.A.M: But you do nothing, right? You could use your privilege and be a helping hand,

CM: I do my best to be an ally, I do my best to take a stand.

A.A.M: Yet we're still dying, being choked out and gunned down,

CM: I understand, but what can I do, what message can I say and spread around?

A.A.M: I... I don't know, I don't have answers, just anger,

CM: Perhaps we can just be kind to each other, be friends instead of a stranger?

A.A.M: How do I know I can trust a friendship with you?

CM: I don't want to be your enemy, just want to be a friend to you.

A.A.M: This black and white shit is making us crazy,

CM: Absolutely, you're right, but we can change that one friendship at a time, and not be lazy.

808s & Heartbreak

Changed My Life (11/25/20 8:22 p.m.)

Okay, so before you read another poem, I had to include this in the book. I wanted to share with you this beautiful recording of art called, "*808s & Heartbreak*," produced, performed and recorded by, well, you know who, Kanye West. I believe it is not only safe to say, but rather necessary to say that Kanye West is arguably one of the most influential artists of all time. I am going to avoid any of the controversial statements and actions Kanye has done throughout his life, I do not want you to be thrown off topic. This is solely about the album and how it changed my life.

So, with that being said, I will continue. Out of all of Kanye's music catalog, *808s & Heartbreak* is my favorite album. It is one of my favorite albums out of all the music I have listened to in my life. For me, I never heard a hip hop album like this before. Prior to this album, I was used to hearing the type of rap music that some would consider to be highly explicit and violent. Not to say that the quality of that style of rap is not great, it most definitely is. But with *808s & Heartbreak*, this was the first time I ever heard an album with this unique and eccentric sound.

I remember when I first listened to the album; well, before I continue with that, I have a confession to make. I was a bit late when it came to Kanye West's music. I mean, I heard some of his songs here and there when I was younger, and then the music started to grow on me. It was not until later on in my life that I acknowledged his greatness. But to continue, when I first heard *808s & Heartbreak*, it just took me to another dimension, another place of being. The sounds of the drums, the minimalistic album cover of the deflated heart-shaped balloon, designed by Virgil Abloh and Willo Perron. But I fell in love with the art cover even more when the deluxe edition was recreated by pop artist Kaws. I loved the "Mickey Mouse gloves" touch on it, as well as the enhanced, contrast color stripes on the side.

Actually, if you look at the cover of my second book, "*Mirrors and Reflections*," you can see that the book cover was inspired by the art cover on *808s and Heartbreak*. But as far as the music on this particular album, my favorite song on this album is "Love Lockdown." I kid you not, I would listen to this song over and over, and over again. There is something about the sound of this song, the lyrics, and the creative use of auto-tone. It is that song, as well as "Say You Will" and "Coldest Winter."

Now with "Coldest Winter," it is actually a sample of a song called, "Memories Fade," performed by the eighties pop group "Tears for Fears," from their album, "*The Hurting*." It is a beautiful song, as well as a beautifully melancholic remake by Kayne West. The reason I say melancholic is because Kanye's version was him paying homage to his late mother, Dr. Donda West. I truly felt Kanye's pain in this particular song; the hurt, the heartbreak, and the reality of it all. I remember walking to work, during the wintertime, and I would suddenly feel the urge to put on my headphones and play this song multiple times. The cold winter chill connected me closer to the song.

I would literally play these three songs from the album in a loop; "Say You Will," "Love Lockdown," and "Coldest Winter." I would listen to all three in random combinations all the time. I can never get bored of them. This may sound weird to you, but to be completely honest with you, this album has helped me grow smarter. The more I listen to it, the smarter I become, and the more creative I become. Let me tell you, I have been listening to *808s & Heartbreak* while I wrote all four of my books. There is a piece of *808s* in all of my books, a piece of inspiration that came from this album. A lot of my poetry was inspired by the sounds that I heard. I would listen to the songs, I would then see colors, I would have visions in my mind, faces I have never seen before, and I would simply write what I envision. I would also listen to Miles Davis as well, and the same process applied.

I know this may sound completely strange, bullshit even. But it is the truth. I just see these visions in my mind and the music helps me see them clearer. It is like how people say when you listen to classical music, such as Mozart or Beethoven, how your studying ability increases. Well, that is what Kanye's music has done for me, believe it or not. Which is why I will continue to listen to it, especially *808s & Heartbreak.* I do not know if you, the reader, have ever heard this album, I know you have heard of Kanye West, that is not even a question, Kanye makes himself well known for sure. But if you have never heard of *808s & Heartbreak,* give it a chance, listen to it, and see for yourself. I do not know if Kanye West will ever see this, but I will leave this in here, "Kanye, thank you for *808s & Heartbreak.* You have changed my life with this album."

"First it was "stop the violence," now it's "stop the virus."

What's A Kanye? (05/08/18)

What's a Kayne without a voice,

Telling the world slavery was just a choice.

A genius mind talking hoodwinked reckless,

Brother forgot our people were in shackles, not a diamond neckless.

What's a Kayne without the eyes,

Free thinking delivers nothing but pricey lies.

Ye screaming "Make America Great Again,"

While fans are praying for him to make a registration late again.

What's a Kanye without a brain,

Calling our brother insane,

When he's lost in the wilderness of fortune and fame.

It can happen to anyone,

No telling what you'd do, walking in the Yeezys of a motherless son.

What's a Kanye without the ears,

Hearing the teacup, seeing the tears.

What's a Kanye without a heart,

A mother and son forever separated, miles apart.

People calling him crazy, bipolar; the ultimate coon,

But how would you feel, waking in the coldest winter night,

Thinking of his best friend, who was gone too soon.

What's a Kanye without a story,

Fighting for his soul and repentance, God be the glory.

What's a Kanye without Roc-a-fella,

Friendships founder; weak propella.

Oops! I said propella; I meant propeller,

You didn't see that, Helen Keller.

What's a Kanye without tomorrow,

A legend, an icon, millions coming together in sorrow.

What is a Kanye without,

Never mind, like Kurt.

World War Humans (11/25/20 9:42 p.m.)

Bullets of questions loaded in the guns of brains,

Headshots, bodies drop, time to mop the blood stains.

Illnesses and disease, ventilation machines and vaccines,

Labels upon labels, the disregard of being human beings.

Fiending fingers feeding false face value,

True misinformation is what separates the nation, don't

believe everything they tell you.

Everyone trying to resell, a capitalistic well,

Stocks rising higher than the flames of hell.

What's a man without machines?

What's an honest rest without dreams?

What's an artist without streams?

2020 is almost history,

2021; hurry, please hurry.

Politics are the circus Olympics,

The votes, the quotes, everything's superfluous and eccentric,

Unapologetic killings, shooters saying they meant it.

Animals kill to live, people live to kill,

People kill the animals; people leave a will.

Oh, we're so twisted in the mind,

Our purpose on this earth is the greatest treasure we have yet

to find.

The world is going nowhere except crazy and derange,

Teenagers shooting protesters, flesh and blood on the street,

it's new the shooting range.

Screens and video games takes the brain away from who's to

blame,

Quadrupled prices for PlayStation and Xbox, don't hate the

player, hate the capital gains.

Gamers on Call of Duty, aiming for the head,

32 rounds created a fatal sound, Breonna Taylor was shot

dead,

Prosecutors fled, charges dropped dead, the bad news began

to spread.

I can't help but think when will people learn,

A year overwhelmed with excessive funerals and urns,

Riots, streets on fire; burn baby, burn.

What to do when the devil wants to play with you?

Lying his music to your ears, he wants to play a song or two.

Human beings; we're not perfect, but we're not helpless at

all,

Lend a helping hand whenever you see someone taking a fall.

One life at a time to save a life from committing crime,

This sentence right here; it's nothing, just needed something

to make it rhyme.

The Afterlife? (11/28/20 4:48 p.m.)

The eyes wide shut, what will we see?

A bright pure white light, or darkness for eternity?

What if we see God, and God says Hi,

Would you ask God, "why do we die?"

Would God ask, "did you enjoy life or no?"

What would you say, "yes or I don't know?"

Do you believe in an afterlife, do you believe in God?

Yes, no, maybe, shoulder shrug or a head nod?

Are you afraid, afraid of eternal rest,

No more life to live, out of this world to an unknown

enigmatic quest.

I'm tired of fear, anxiety just go away for good,

We should enjoy our lives, as satisfied as we possibly could.

Once it's over, it's over; never to return,

Ashes to ashes, dust to dust, burials and urns,

What did you gain in your life, what legacy did you earn?

What will you remember, what did you learn?

What will be your final song, your final words, when it is

your turn?

"To be great, you can't just sit there and wait. But you have to be patient with the results of your perseverance."

The Good Life with Gray Hair (11/28/20 6:18 p.m.)

A senior citizen she is, older than the bench she sits on at the
park,
No glasses as she sees clearly; the birds, people, and dogs
giving loud barks.
As she sits, she watches her granddaughter at play,
Swinging away; slides and seesaws on such a beautiful day.
Her granddaughter says, "watch me Granny Mae, watch me
down the slide,"
A precious moment, her emotions she tried to hide.
She's so grateful, a cancer survivor, still kicking at eighty,
She calls over her granddaughter, just to say, "I love you
Katie."
"I love you too Granny Mae," she then runs back to her dad,
She's been a widow for fifteenth years now, every so often
she misses her husband and feels sad.
She sits and she wonders, how much time is left for herself,
She gave up meat and drinks, as true health is true wealth.
She wants to live, live long enough to see her granddaughter
grow more and more,
She's not quite ready to knock, knock on heaven's door.
Yet she sits with a smile on her face,
Her life is now a marathon, too tired to race.

Her gray hair blowing in the wind, Katie blows Granny Mae
a kiss,
At her age, every day is a blessing, a gift with a twist.
It's time for Katie's nap, they call it a day,
Katie takes a light fall, Granny Mae says, "Katie, you're
okay?"
Katie's dad picks her up, brushed the dirt off her little
shoulders,
Granny Mae is too slow to get up, by the minute she grows
older and older.
Katie's dad helps his mother up and says, "you're ready to go
home mom?"
She responded, "yes, and I appreciate you bringing me out
here, I love you Tom."
Life must not be so bad when you get older,
Maybe your body shrinks, blood gets a little colder.
But as long as you live, let the good life turn gray,
Enjoy life to the fullest, be alive and happy like Granny Mae.

Violin with My Heart (11/29/20 6:04 p.m.)

My life is falling apart,

Yet you don't catch the pieces with your colossal heart.

I'm trapped in depression,

Heartbroken lessons,

Class been in session,

The broken pieces of my heart escaped in recession.

Distant measures of my romantic treasures,

Watch your step as my heart's all over the floor, yet you

stepped on it at your pleasure.

You dismiss my delicious kisses,

I need a genie to grant my wishes,

A genius mind I possess, my hunger grows vicious.

Give me a chance with a forgiving dance,

Your beauty is salvation at first glance.

Drive me insane with your yes, no, maybe games,

Back and forth moments, time tasted but wasted, what a

shame.

I have more thoughts than autumn leaves falling,

Respond to my text, stop the digital stalling.

I just want you to show me the way I never seen,

I want to start on another path, fresh and oh so clean.

A traffic of words in my brain,

Trying to brush them like my hair, but I'm going against the

grain.

Love is the fortune, time is the fame,

Let's be famous together, all over the world in jet planes,

Violin with my heart, you're great at it, but please, oh please,

stop playing.

We're Food (11/29/20 11:22 p.m.)

Living in a land that can't be trusted,

Dead meat in a systematic crust of injustice,

Peace of mind, frozen in time, political liars saying, "trust us."

Extra, extra; cheese all about it,

Blood leaks, looking like pizza sauce,

Tears after tears, so sorry for you loss.

Soldiers in the night, praying to make it home,

Dog eat dog world, people skinned to the bone,

The youth taking rain checks to their tombstones.

Billions of breathing flesh, the battle of cattle,

So many secrets in this world, social media; fairytale land to tattle.

We're food on a plate,

Time for a remedy diet, before it is too late.

"Laws should be looked upon as an everlasting molding of obedience to our civilization."

The Breakup
(12/1/20 1:58 a.m.)

<u>Boyfriend</u>: Hey, thanks for meeting up with me,

<u>Girlfriend</u>: Hey, no problem, you ordered my favorite coffee I see.

<u>BF</u>: Yea, I figured I'd do something to make you smile one last time before you go,

<u>GF</u>: I'm so sorry, but there is something I want you to know.

<u>BF</u>: What exactly is that?

<u>GF</u>: I thought about it, and I'll give you another chance and take you back.

<u>BF</u>: Oh, I wasn't expecting you to tell me that, why the sudden change of heart?

<u>GF</u>: We've been together for so long, it's been so strong, too strong to fall apart.

<u>BF</u>: I see, but I have a confession to make, I saw your smile, now I may see you cry,

<u>GF</u>: Oh God please, not another secret, not another lie.

<u>BF</u>: I'm terribly sorry, but the bond we have, that bond must break,

<u>GF</u>: Why? Why can't we fight through this? Let's fight it, whatever it takes.

<u>BF</u>: Please don't make this difficult, please just go,

<u>GF</u>: Why? What is wrong? I don't want to let you go; no, no, no.

BF: Stop, lower your voice, you're making a scene,

GF: Why are you doing this? I can't let you go, you're the man of my dreams.

BF: You just have to move on with your life, forget about me,

GF: How could I just forget about seven straight years with you, please?

BF: I'm so sorry, but there's, there's someone else I'm seeing now,

GF: Oh, wow, I see, so you just want me to forget us, dismiss all the who, what, when, and how?

BF: Yes, and I can't be your friend, Sam doesn't like to share,

GF: Sam? You better not be referring to Sam, my cousin? Don't you dare.

BF: I think it's time I go, and yes, it's your cousin,

GF: Sam is married, Sam has a husband.

BF: That's news to me, just didn't mention a word,

GF: Her husbands in the army, he's striving to be a full bird.

BF: Well, that's not your concern is it, it's still over, we're done,

GF: You're both low down pieces of shit; be my guess, have fun.

BF: So, I guess you're going to go home and cry like a baby?

GF: No, I guess what I have to do now is go to the clinic and get rid of our unborn baby.

BF: Oh dear God, what?

GF: Yea, I'm carrying your child, that's why I didn't what to break up, but go, go back to your slut.

BF: You can't do this, that's my seed,

GF: Well, you can't have it all; you're so selfish and dishonest, filled with greed.

BF: Don't kill our baby, I'm begging you on my knees,

GF: I'm just stuck between a rock and a hard place with you now, too numb to trust, too far to believe.

BF: Please, don't; what can I do to make it right?

GF: Call my cousin Sam and tell her goodbye and goodnight.

BF: Is there anything else? I'll do what it takes to make up,

GF: Make up? I'm afraid that's not possible, all you can do now is be a father to our child, but as for you and me, we, we must break up.

"Normality is only effective when you have control. However, the colossal population of humanity makes normalization cease to exist."

D.R.E.A.M.　　　　　(12/1/20　2:42 a.m.)

Drugs ruined everyone around me,

Get the pipe, crack cocaine kills y'all.

A mini heroine puddle, boiling in a silver spoon,

Needle through the veins, poison to the brain, overdose,

gone too soon.

Light a blunt, weed smoke on a hunt for your brain cells,

Laced the blunt, taste the skunk, bricks in the trunk, now

you're going to jail.

Raising hell behind those bars,

Razors are the fingernails that leave those scars.

Pill popping and lean sipping,

Paranoid, dope fiend leans and tripping.

Zombies on the streets like the walking dead,

Dealers on the corner working for the feds,

All over the nation, an everlasting spread.

Drugs ruined everyone around me,

Get the rocks, crack cocaine kills y'all.

Scratching the itches,

Crackheads and snitches,

Homecoming queens became dope fiend witches.

A devotion to the destructive potions,

Smoking that glass wand, frozen emotions.

Stashes on the ground,

Abandoned houses were bodies are found,

Everyone had that phone call, hearing those crying sounds,

The Devil put the peddle to the metal, winning this race, he

said, give me my crown."

This isn't a black, brown, or white thing,

A rich or poor thing,

Anyone alive can catch this disease, all it takes is that first

pinch and sting.

Come back for more, now your arms filled with holey sores,

No need to knock, death has an open door.

Nightmares, blind-eyed citizens who don't stare, don't care,

don't bare to realize the world isn't fair.

Blind to the pain of the fiends,

Step over the fact that they're human beings.

Wrap their arms, pop the vein,

Stop the war, end the drug game.

Drugs Ruined Everyone Around Me,

Get the pills, crack cocaine kills y'all.

"If you love Wu Tang Clan, you'll understand."

A Writer's Block

(12/1/20 10:46 p.m.)

I can't write, I can't think,

A sudden drought of thoughts, no brainstorm,

no rain for my brain cells to drink.

No ideas, no visions, no words, I'm stuck,

I'm trying to write a line, but I'm getting no such luck.

Do I have nothing to say, nothing to write,

Nothing in my brain, not on the left or the right?

Empty notebook, nothing to bleed,

Empty notebook, nothing to read.

So much to talk about,

But unable to chalk it out.

"I'm not looking for the perfect woman,
I'm looking for a woman who is so
enough, that I would forget what
perfection is."

Pillow Talk

(12/1/20 10:55 p.m.)

I opened my eyes, grateful for another day,

I see her sleeping face, a kiss to bae.

Then another, and another, she awakes and smiles,

We sleep so close, but when we dream, we're separated for miles.

Playing with her hair, my fingers caught in her tangled curls,

God I love her smile, her teeth are of alabaster pearls,

I love her hugs and kisses, she's my favorite girl.

A whisper to my concerned ear,

I have her trust as she gives me her secrets and fears.

She tells me her past, prays our love will last,

We take it slow; we don't move so fast.

Her vanilla scented cuddles, gives me comfort and joy,

We talk our plans of children, one name for a girl and boy.

Under the covers we go, our bodies create blanket mountains,

Laying sideways like Buddha, with snow blanketing the mountains.

She wraps her arms and legs around me, holds me so tight,

Not much more to talk about, just a kiss, "I love you,"

another kiss, and goodnight.

"If money becomes dishonest, people's mentality will also become dishonest, which will then cause a dishonest society."

The Guitar Man (12/4/20 11:28 p.m.)

Chelsea boots walking, Denim jacket and jeans,

The weight of his guitar on his back, his new single hit ten

million streams.

He goes to his local park, sits on a bench and plays a song,

Then a group of delinquents pulled out their deadly

instruments, they didn't come to play along.

One said, "Hand over the guitar, and I'll spare your life,"

Guitar man said, "be cool guy, I got a kid and pregnant wife."

"Just give me the Goddamn guitar," he said with malice,

He cautiously hands the guitar over, thinking, "I'm not

making it back, I love you Casey, Molly, and Alice."

One delinquent snatched the guitar out of his hands, three ran

off, one stayed behind,

The remaining delinquent said, "I should put a bullet between

your eyes, buried deep into your mind."

Guitar man said, "all I have in this world is my family,

I wrote many songs and won some Grammys.

If you could just spare my life, I feel your pain,

Save whatever goodness you have left, cherish what

remains."

The delinquent said, "shut the hell up, you don't know my

pain,"

Guitar man responded, "why, because my complexion is different than yours, because I have fortune and fame?"
The delinquent said, "hell yea, my dad left us all, I had to be my family's superhero with a cape,"
Guitar man said, "well, my dad left us too, but before he left, he introduced my mom to rape."
The delinquent looked with guilty regret,
Thinking only his life was a struggle, until someone experienced worst, someone he just met.
Delinquent said, "Forgive me man, I made a, I made a terrible mistake,"
Guitar man said, "A guitar can be replaced, not a life, change your ways before it's too late."
The delinquent lowered the gun and ran off; said not one word, but in his mind he thanked the guitar man,
A lonely tear cries down guitar man's face, thinking to himself, "I think I have a new fan."

Girl Surviving Thirteen (12/5/20 2:10 a.m.)

Her innocence, naivety in her consciousness, youth in her
veins,

She wakes up into her smartphone, social media
programming her brain.

She got likes, but wants more,

She wants to ride her bike to the store,

But wait; she gets a creepy knock on her bedroom door.

A familiar knock, she knows who's out there,

A wicked mother, she says to her daughter, "let me in, I need
to cut your hair."

Scared girl, being used as a slave,

She's drowning, can't swim, trapped by these masculine
waves.

Fragile child she is, a mother pimping her kid,

Dirty old men, toothless grins, shame on their bids.

They have a winner, who is an ultimate sinner,

He requests that they starve her, he wants her a little thinner.

Down the basement her mother takes her, locks her down in
the thickest of chains,

What does this do to a teenage girl's brain? She's trying her
best, preventing to go insane.

Her first John was a man, middle-aged perverted man named
Kevin,

She had her first encounter with him when she was...When
she was only eleven.

She's desperately suffering from hunger, energy at an all-
time low,

Hallucinations in the dark, yet a spark begins to grow.

Was it a dream, was it a God, did she die and say, "I can't do
this anymore?"

Did she look up the stairs and see heaven's door?

No, it was the basement door, police did a raid, down the
stairs they come, in a group of four.

One said, "Lord have all mercy, are you okay?"

She looked at him and said, "I...I wouldn't have made it
another day."

Cop called it in and said, "we obtain another one in the
basement, that makes twelve,"

Twelve teenage girls pimped and drugged out in this living
hell.

Out the hell house they take her, in the ambulance she rides,

Slipping in and out of consciousness, she saw little body
bags, two of the girls were tragically sold to suicide.

She cries, and cries, and cries herself into a deep sleep,

She dreams, in a world of honey-dipped pinecones and
billowy sheep,

All who were there had happiness, not one teary weep.

She saw fireflies, collecting them in a glass jar,

Some were close, some were too far,

In the dream, she had no bruises, no pain, no scars.

What a dreamland, a fairy flew to the girl and waved her wand,

The fairy said come with me, come to my magic pond.

The little girl went and saw her reflection in the water,

The fairy said, "it is not your fault, it is not your fault my daughter."

The girl looks at her reflection, her dropping tears creates the loneliest ripples,

Teardrops after teardrops, trickle after trickle.

The fairy comes near, waving her wand back and forth asking her, "are you okay?"

The girl responded, "yes, I love it here, oh please can I stay?"

The fairy, saddened by the girl's innocence, she doesn't know her whereabouts,

The fairy said, "oh my daughter, it is not your time, you must be returned back to your mundane route.

The girl grew confused as the wand kept waving left to right,

Until the girl came to, she realized that it was a doctor, waving back and forth with his flashlight.

The little girl, with all her might, asked, "what happened, where's the wand and stardust?"

The doctor said, "baby, your heart stopped beating for seven minutes, we thought you left us."

The little girl thought to herself, "perhaps I died and went to heaven,"
As she looked to the hospital clock with hazy vision, the time had the p.m. version of 11:11.
The girl planted the seeds of hope and faith, surrounded by the growth of healing,
Far away from her inhumane mother, what a glorious feeling.
Thirteen; the year that she survived,
Love and support are what's missing, her hunger for it, she's so deprived.
Will you love her, she needs it madly,
Life's a stage, we're all characters at play, let us pray she has a healing finale.

Little Jewish Boy in the Ghetto   (12/5/20 4:28 p.m.)

Playing in the Warsaw ghetto streets, the little Jewish boy,

Poverty stricken, with wood and cloth, he made his own toy.

Forced to live in slums, no sewage or water, how can one
forget that smell?

If you call this living, this was a living hell.

Children smuggling food through the cracks of ghetto walls,

Children begging in order to survive; no mom or dad, no
family at all.

Multiple Jewish families in one apartment; starvation, people
sicken with disease,

Winter has arrived, orphan children on the streets begin to
freeze.

But this little Jewish boy had a family, a family of five,

The Nazi soldiers invades the ghetto, very few made it out
alive.

Children and the elderly, thrown in trucks and gas vans,

Treated as if they were nothing, kicked around likeempty
tomato cans.

Objects thrown as they walk, Germans taunting oppression,

Walking in lines with luggage, The Schutzstaffel staring with
demonic possessions,

Confiscated mountains of family photos, jewelry, shoes and
other sacred possessions.

Bullets to brains, blood stains splattered on concrete walls,

Hiding from SS in pianos, the floor, and bedroom walls,

Lined up; they aimed, they fired, like dominos they fall.

The little Jewish boy and his family, placed in a crowded train
car, taken out of the ghetto,

To Auschwitz-Birkenau they go, holding his mother's hand,
soldier screamed in German, "Let her go! Let her go!"

Little Jewish boy, smacked to the ground as he said, "Mommy,
daddy, don't leave,"

Soldiers with broad shoulders took him away, sat him down and
said, "roll up your sleeve."

They dismissed his name, tattooed numbers on his arm,

Branded, stranded with other kids, the malicious harm.

So many kids, everyone with numerical stamps,

Stars, pinned-stripped jackets and hats, the destination
of concentration and extermination camps.

Nothing but skin on top of his skull, as they shaved his head,

At twelve years old, he sees children and parents, shot dead.

Hell on earth is what he sees, what he lives throughout the
years,

Traumatized eyes as he saw a man's brains blown throughout
the ears.

Little Jewish boy made it to thirteen, forced labor for their
brutal institution,

A nation of annihilation, as the Nazis prepare for the "Final
Solution."
Redrum and then some, stepping in bloody puddles on the
ground,
Bullet after bullet, bodies upon bodies, the screams, he can't
escape the nightmarish sounds.
Wooden bunk beds, stacked and starved to death,
The boy saw so many, taking their last breath.
The absence of flesh, nothing but skin and bones,
Buried naked human beings, no caskets, no tombstones.
Tear drops on the unmarked graves; the boy can't stop
crying,
Human beings placed in ovens; men, women, and children
frying.
So many shootings the boy eye witnessed, lined them up one
by one,
The worst he saw was a pregnant woman, shot execution
style, right in front of her son,
Then her son was killed by the gas chamber, brick walls,
nowhere to run.
The boy's surviving, but the bodies were rising,
Nazi soldiers raised their slanted arms high, to the Devil they
were idolizing.
There was nowhere to run, but the little Jewish boy was able
to hide,

Hidden by prisoners, who were already on the inside,

But later found out his mother, father, sister and baby brother,

were all members of the genocide.

But he's safe, he survived, fortunate that he's not alone,

The little Jewish boy became a man, an old man, with a large

family of his own.

Every year he takes his family to the site, to pay homage to

millions, and to his family he lost,

In his old mind he said, "Dear God, may we never, ever

experience another Holocaust.

"Even though the little Jewish boy in this poem is based on a fictional character, this story is based on true, tragic events. This particular poem, it took me some time to write, as it was extremely difficult to create the imagery without being as graphic. But after doing much research, after seeing the documentaries and video footage, there was just no way around it. I had to include what actually happened to millions of people, Jewish families, human beings. I want to say this again; to be very clear, in absolutely no way am I trying to make light of such an inhumane, tragic event such as the Holocaust. Please forgive me if any of it was too heartbreaking to read through. I wrote this poem because I believe it is imperative that people, especially younger generations, know some of the history, and to know that this really did happen. This was one of my most difficult poems to write and get through. I know this poem comes nowhere close to the whole history, but I hope it was enough of the truth."

-Jordan Wells

Life My Wife

(12/5/20 5:56 p.m.)

Life is the love of my life,

I get on one knee; I make you my wife.

You are my dream come true, a gift from the highest,

You're so beautiful, to have you, I'm so grateful, I just want

to sigh.

Life: I want to grow old with you,

You're the only one I'll ever have, once it's over, I'm

through.

Just you and me, til death do us part,

I am thankful for you, every day you touch my heart.

As long as I have you, I am alive and well,

Yet I'm still trying to figure out what you are, are you a

dream or a spell,

What is my ultimate purpose, I guess time with you will tell.

"Do not start over but start forward. That should be the new message. Start forward with your life."

I Am Gun (2/13/14; edited on 12/23/19)

I am the quickest killer ever known to man,

I can kill anyone or anything, give me your hand.

My bullet soldiers are what I use,

I can order them in any direction, but you must choose.

I was born and made in China; in case you didn't know,

Now I'm everywhere, like water, I flow.

Don't know my exact date of birth, know I'll never die,

Killed millions since day one; no remorse, I don't cry.

I am a Hollywood mogul, an idol to the music of rap,

I don't know why I'm so unique; I'm giving the living a dirt nap.

If only you can see peoples' faces once I show them mine,

It's like they can't move, can't talk, frozen in a non-Disney time.

I am a way of life, or should I say death,

I observed so many lives taking their last breath.

I am the master instrument of instant incidents,

Mass and school shootings, innocent bodies, bloody craters and dents.

Some call me protection, keeping me in their nightstands,

Others call me a weapon if I fall into the wrong hands.

Ban me, have me deported; I'll leave and never come back,

Been through too many wars, genocide, suicides, deadly attacks.

I've seen it all, till this day I can't believe this life is real,

I don't understand why people use me to kill.

America, oh America, why do you love me so much?

Is it the sounds, the smell, the taste, the grip, or the touch?

Shootings every single day; some survive, some win,

I always wondered why my trigger is shaped like the Amazon grin.

To the good, I am bad, to the bad I am good,

With my double-barrel shotgun eyes, I clearly can see we're all misunderstood.

April to October   (2/18/20)

Her mother she loves, her mother the dancer,

A kiss to her hairless skull, momma is battling with cancer.

Once a very little girl, seeing her momma beautifully dance,

Holding her hand; kissing her arm, this is her only chance.

"Dance with me baby, come dance with your mother,"

You're only blessed one mother on this earth, after that, there's no other.

Momma once picked her up, she spread her arms like wings and pretended to fly,

Daughter picks up momma; falling from weaken legs, momma crying, "I don't want to die."

Daughter lays in bed with momma, humming their favorite song,

A bond that is so strong, but soon won't be for long.

A daughter, not yet crossed the finish line of pre-teen years,

She remembers her momma on that stage, standing ovations, clapping hands, all the cheers.

"My darling April," her momma begins to talk,

"The leaves are falling, please, oh please can we go for a walk?"

"Momma you're too weak, I can't carry you, I'm just a little girl,"

"But I want to dance one last time, in the autumn leaves; just one last twirl."

"I'll dance for you momma; I'll dance while you're in bed,"

"Okay baby, dance as the little angel you are, you are beautiful as I always said."

Humming their favorite song again; April dances and twirls, little girl at play,

Disconnected duet, momma's voice peacefully fades away.

April screams her favorite word, three commas:

"MOMMA, MOMMA, MOMMA, MOMMAAAAA!!!!!

Reflection of a Shadow   (12/9/20 11:02 p.m.)

Imagine a black and white picture, he walks in lonesomeness
by the lake,
Breaking of a new dawn, waiting for the world to awake.
His footsteps on the concrete ground,
Bird chirping echoes in a duet with cricket sounds.
Natures cadence, the wind sends a breeze,
A morning chill, minor sniffles and a sneeze.
He stands by the lake, only seeing his shadowy reflection,
A dark figure of himself in the water, no face, no direction.
An unclear purpose, he's lost and alone,
Ripples through the lake as he launches another stone.
Of course, the pain is by the absence of a woman who left,
Her absent presence is of the absence of breath.
Like no air in his lungs,
No love songs to be sung,
No wedding bells to be rung.
How could something feel so perfect be neglected?
Years of what seemed true, but the second chance was
rejected,
I guess his heart was under-protective.
Their love's conclusion became a heart-aching contusion,
She calls, she text, then she ignores, swelling confusion.
The sun's peaking in its usual enlightened space,

The look of a shiny mole lingered and floating through the sky's face.
Watch as the sun paints the colorful reflection of his face in the lake,

He may never fall in love again, what an absolute heartbreak.

Until another reflection cast beside his own,

It was her, his brain said stay away, but his heart said welcome home.

Instead of stones, her teardrops created ripples in the lake,

He said, "If I'm dreaming, I hope I never awake.

He traded his forgiveness for her hugs and apologies,

He said, "You're my moon, my stars," as he believes in astrology.

She kissed him on the cheek and said, "Can I come home?"

He doesn't want to grow old living alone,

He said okay, with a humbling, satisfying tone.

Like Teenagers

(12/12/20 4:00 p.m.)

Feels like two teenagers, stuck in our youth,

Smiling for a four-time flash, kissing in the photo booth.

You grabbed my hand, the way you look at me and smile,

Step by step, you're still holding my hand after we walked a
mile.

Your soft cushioned lips don't say word, not one letter,

Your lips pressed against mine, my worst day, you make it
better.

I worship the footprints you leave in the wet sand,

You make me feel so young, but I'm a boy who became a
man.

I love how you run and leap into my open arms,

I hope you like the necklace with our picture in the charm.

Our popcorn fights when we watch movies,

All it took was a tap on your shoulder and I said, "excuse
me?"

Instantly fell in love like it was no tomorrow,

Our love will remain young forever, even though our flesh is
time borrowed.

We share our secrets, we share ice cream,

Our cuddles are a sacred intimate huddle, we make the cutest
team.

Thank you for being on my team,

Having you in my life is the realest dream.

I think of you every day, every night,

You are the good in my goodbyes and good nights.

It's so strange to love someone who was once a stranger,

But whatever, let's continue to love each other, and stay

young like teenagers.

Unconditional Identity   (12/12/20 11:24 p.m.)

A look in the mirror, what is seen,

Man, woman, or them, not in between.

Society fears what it doesn't understand,

Unwilling to educate, no knowledge to expand.

People judge, the disrespect, the phobia and shame,

Don't put a label on a human being, put respect on their

name.

Life is hard enough for people abandoned by family and

friends,

Questions with confused facial expressions, when will the

torment end?

Gender identity, neutral is the remedy,

They and them pronouns for enby.

Love could win if you don't judge within,

Some are simply fearless, unapologetic comfort in their own

skin.

If you're ever kicked to the curve of a street,

Don't cry, brush yourself off and stand on your own two feet.

You'll be okay even if you see yourself in a different way,

No matter what, you're still human at the end of the day.

Real love will find you whenever you're lost,

Always be careful, pay attention, no matter the cost.

"Rumors in today's world are digital cancer cells metastasizing all over the social fabric of our morality."

"Social Media is the snitch industry."

Women's Rights   (12/17/20 1:44 p.m.)

Yes, a menstrual cycle will make her leak,

Once a month, five to seven days out of a week.

It is natural for her to bleed,

She has the right to be out in public and breastfeed.

Men take away her right to abort,

Yet men's unsolicited seeds are planted in her reproductive

resort.

Unfair world to a woman's existence,

Progressive aggressiveness, women constantly having to

show resistance.

Men treating women like toys, like pieces of degraded meat,

When was the last time you saw a man offer a woman his

seat?

Society placing women in the worst position,

Some are cisgender; some have to make a risky transition.

Women's opinions in sports result in sarcastic remarks,

Women's rights are left abandoned, missing in the masculine

dark.

A man's world, how does women survive,

The abuse, the rapes, the molestations, yet they're still strong

and alive.

Women's physical strength is no match for man,

But women's tolerance to contractions, men could never understand.

Women still marching in streets, demanding their rights,

Step by step towards equality as they finally see the light.

They march, they speak, they cry every step of the way,

Protesting for equal rights, votes, and equal pay.

Mother to sons and daughters,

The power of life arrives during the breaking of her water.

Women's rights, they can't be ignored, can't be unsaid,

It's time to resurrect chivalry, because chivalry is dead.

Treat a woman with respect, a young boy's life lesson,

Never treat her like property, women are no man's possession.

Women are precious, life painfully comes through them,

To all women, protect your rights, before man foolishly tries to remove them.

Unsolicited Genius (12/16/20 10:26 p.m.)

You may never care to know me,

It's okay because there's nothing that you owe me.

Refusal and rejections, wishing me the "best of luck,"

But deep down, I don't think they ever gave a fuck.

It sucks but I guess I understand,

But I can't wait for traditional yes or no's, I can't wait for fans.

My creativity is at an all-time high,

My work is telling my truth, even when I lie.

When I cry, my thoughts grow sharper than thorns,

When I die, my words will live on and on.

They can't except, it's unsolicited, such a shame,

I don't care for the views, likes, or fame,

There's no such thing in this capital game.

I turn average words into genius thoughts,

I turn your twenty-two dollars into a brilliant bought.

You don't have to give me credit, you already gave your credit card when you pressed "add to cart,"

Your purchase was made, I thank you in advance from the bottom of my grateful heart.

Have your reviews for your YouTube views,

Subliminal messages lie deep, hidden clues.

I'm going to make you think,

Teardrops when your eyes blink,

I write so much, my pens lack of ink.

Some call it unsolicited, I call it a gift,

I have the best poetry of ALL TIME, but Imma let you finish

Taylor Swift.

I'm going to keep writing until they can't stop writing about

me,

The hard work will speak for itself; it will speak of me.

All I did was believed in me,

All has paid off; much was relieved in me.

Don't call it unsolicited, call it genius,

When it's all set and done; your kids just might use me for

their thesis.

She Danced with the Devil Part 2 <small>(12/17/20 1:15 a.m.)</small>

She's running for her life, killer in a full moon night,

Anxiety attack in the pitch black, the killer is nowhere in sight.

Incoming! Killer gives her an open-handed skelp,

She screams, nothing but chilly echoes of help.

"Help someone, please," is all she can scream,

Running like hell, fear is scuba diving in her bloodstreams.

The woods are a good place to hide, or so she thought,

She hides behind a thick barked tree, praying she doesn't get caught.

The frosted breath exiting out the blistering doors of her lips,

A snow-covered branch hidden in plain sight, what a scream, what a trip.

Planked in the snow,

But the killer is now a no show,

Quick thoughts in her mind, she's thinking, "where, where did he go?"

Snow and trees are all she sees,

Shivers are delivered to her body, cold crawling on her hands and knees.

Too afraid to scream, killer may be near and deadly dear,

Twisting her head to look around, panoramic view with fear.

The same tree branch that gave her a trip,

Has now evolved into her weapon, she holds on with the
tightest grip.

She got off her knees,

Unleashed a random sneeze,

Her grip grows tighter and tighter, she begins to squeeze.

An eerie sound of creepy whistles invades her eardrums,

Will this be a night of survival, or a night of redrum?

Still holding on to the branch, ready to swing away,

The whistles come again; the killer is ready to play.

She screams, "I know you're out there you sick fuck,"

A voice responded saying, "don't be afraid, I just want your
head for good luck."

Her eyes never opened so wide before,

Afraid she'll be a body of blood squirts and gore.

She stepped out into the open space,

Courageous woman as she says, "show me your face."

All she hears are the killer's footsteps, crushing the million
flakes of glittery snow,

Out of the dark he emerged, a grin only a demon could show.

She's shaking with the branch in her hands,

No match for him; six foot, five inches is the height he
stands.

Her terrified face, the killer moves towards her, giant
footprints,

Back pedal after back pedal, she throws the branch at the
killer and began to sprint.

Running as fast as a nightmare ever made her run,

A quick turn, there's a man, with a double barrel shotgun.

He says, "get down now, I got him in sight,"

BOOM! BOOM! Dear killer, say good night.

She lays on the icy ground, her hair all in her face,

This man has saved her life, he's ended the killer's chase.

She looks at the man and said, "thank you, I thought I was
going to die,"

He said, "I kept hearing your screams and your cries."

The killer has been shot twice, her and the man goes to his
truck,

They drive off, he gets on his radio and said, "someone
answer! What the fuck?"

Then an answer came through, but it was that same creepy
whistle,

"Uh oh" was the look they gave each other; victory received
an early dismissal.

The killer is still on the loose, alive and well,

What will it take for them to send this demon back to hell?

"I refuse to second guess my opinions based on the majority of others disagreeing with my opinions."

She Felt Complete Again (12/17/20 3:26 p.m.)

Fully grown woman, with a mind of her own,

Her hands covering her eyes as she looks in the mirror,

embarrassed by her body tone.

Love handles that she can't handle,

Her mid-section never recovered from c-section; her waist

looks like a melted candle.

Men use to take her out, now they show up very late,

The more she loses her figure, the more she's stood up on

dates.

She hates to shower, washing her shapeless frame,

She used to be her town's beauty pageant winner,

She loved when they called her name.

Hard to keep a toned body, birthing a daughter and two sons,

Her ex-husband would always tease her saying, "how are you

thick but have the flattest buns?"

Her self-esteem was just about dead,

Every night, tear-soaking pillows as she laid in bed.

Until one morning she woke up and saw the light,

The light of her phone, a notification in her sight.

A video notification of a woman who had a Brazilian butt lift,

Inspiration for her consciousness, her self-esteem would

uplift.

She reached out and researched, emailing surgeons saying,
"what's up doc?"
Her jewelry is filled with karats, diamond rocks.
By rabbit foot luck, the pawnshop gave her a fortune for her
diamond rocks,
Made her down payments, now in the waiting room, staring
at the clock.
The doctor walks in, consultation mixed with her tears,
The doctor assured her to stay calm and dismiss all her fears.
She told doc, "I just want to be beautiful again, sexy and
desirable,"
The doc responded, "once I'm done with you, your body will
be so admirable."
The curves of her lips began to bend as she molds a smile on
her relived face,
The doctor convinced her that she's in the right place.
The day has come, under the knife she goes,
A couple of prayers, injected anesthesia, her eyes began to
close.
The doctors begin the procedure, cuts through layers of skin,
The Epidermis, the dermis, thick hypodermic, now he's in.
Transferred fat cells,
Recovery will be a living hell.
Breast augmentation is next on her list,
Lip fillers and Botox, she can't resist.

A LONELY ROSE

Months gone by, barely able to sit,

But miraculously, her old clothes are starting to fit. Glancing

at the mirror and bragging, saying, "oh my God, who is

this?"

Pose after pose, thinking in her mind, "I'm now a Goddess."

She looks better than ever, going on shopping sprees,

Her body pics going viral on the gram, men and women

commenting, "OMG, marry me?"

She's loving the love, and haters are a must,

The old her is dead, ashes to eyelashes, dust to lust.

She's walking down the street, feeling oh so good about

herself,

Her spirit is alive and well, at peace with her mental health.

Maybe for some, it makes all the difference in the world,

She's no longer that fragile, scared, insecure little girl.

*To be clear, by no means am I trying to encourage any
women to have work done to their bodies. That is a personal
choice on their behalf. This as well is a fictional character.*

-Jordan Wells

"Caress my possessions to manifest,

Dressed in stress, tears won't let me rest,

Wrestling with my fears,

Paranoid roads got me swiftly switching

gears.

Who killed love? All I see are likes."

Who Are You?   (12/18/20 7:32 p.m.)

He's running after her, down a cold and quiet city block,
He screams her name; she stops in front of the midnight
clock.
He catches up and tries to hug his apology onto her, but she
sheds away,
He tries again but she cries, "get away."
His struggle with his hazy love for her is breaking them apart,
He's being unclear with her, and it is breaking her heart.
The mixture of tears and makeup is giving her such a
melancholy face,
She says to him, "just leave me alone, go back to your place."
But he stays, he begs, begging for her forgiveness,
Yet her solid-heavy doubts tell her not to relive this.
She walks away from him, down the subway stairs,
He follows, all the pride he swallows, sits across from her on
the train, and stares.
He stares at her frowning Mona Lisa,
He looked at her and said, "I'm so sorry Lisa."
Lisa wiped her sniffling nose with her one and only tissue,
Lisa finally asked him, "what is your Goddamn issue?"
His face grew quiet and confused,
Knowing that what he's putting her through, is emotional
abuse.

He tells her, "I just need time to think,"

He then stares again, blink, after blink, after blink.

"Who are you then?" Lisa asked with her crying face,

Fast pacing heartbeat, as if the train and his heart were in a race.

He said, "I'm in love with you, I truly am,

I just don't know if I can have you, along with my friends and fam."

The train reached its last stop, end of the ride,

Lisa said, "tell them the truth, you're too alive to hide."

He looks at Lisa, he doesn't know what to say,

Lisa asked him, "what, do you think they'll assume that you're gay?"

His anger boils, not to Lisa but to himself,

He's afraid to reveal his truth, his romantic stealth.

Walking down the street with Lisa, he kicked over a bag of cans,

His truth: he's in love with a woman, a woman who is trans.

A woman of trans experience is who Lisa is, but who is he?

Afraid of the world's judgements but living his truth shall set him free.

He wants to be free, free with Lisa, but his fear is so strong,

He's hurting Lisa, deep down he knows he's dead wrong.

He held Lisa tight in the chilly winds of the city,

He said, "I hate hiding how I feel, in such a judgmental
society."
She looked up to him, wiped the tears from his eyes,
Then she said, "don't kill your truth and then feed it to lies,
There's nothing wrong with loving who you love, let your
spirit rise."

"Thinking/brainstorming is like fishing. The fish are your ideas, your thoughts, your opinions and philosophies on life. We have thousands of thoughts and ideas swimming in our minds daily. We have to catch them while we have a chance."

A Homeless Heart (12/19/20 12:30 a.m.)

No one cares to see her, she's like a living ghost,

The cold winter has arrived, searching to find the warmest

coats.

Pushing her shopping cart that's absent of food,

She pleasantly asked for monetary help, but some people's

hearts beat so crude.

She wasn't born in this dead-end situation,

Let's go back a decade, when she had a more professional

presentation.

A career woman she was, business suits and a briefcase,

Business boomed, then business was doomed, she lost her

case.

Lawsuits after lawsuits, her fortune went down the drain,

Foreclosed homes, the leeches she called family left her

alone, the pain injected in her brain.

Nowhere to go, it all came full circle,

She prayed for it all back, she prayed for a miracle.

It happened so fast, and now she's here,

How long will this last? Forever she fears.

Minute by minute, she asks for help, dollars or coins,

Until one person actually stepped to her at a bench and asked,

"may I join?"

She said, "okay, my name is Rebecca,"

He responded saying, "Nice to meet you, I'm Cal, I'm from Tribeca."

Cal noticed her shivers, and the echoes of pain from her growling stomach,

He said, "it sounds like you haven't eaten in a while, let's get some food in you quick."

Her gratefulness showed on her face,

A conversation grew between them, she shared her stories about how she lost her money and her case.

Cal felt much sorrow, but Rebecca didn't want his pity,

He bought a brand-new coat for her, to keep warm in the windy city.

As she was walking away, Cal said, "Rebecca, wait!"

She turned around and he said, "This must be fate."

He offered her a place to stay, a warm place to lay her head,

With tears in her eyes, she said, "you mean I get to have my own bed?"

Rebecca couldn't ask for anything more,

Overwhelmed with gratitude, she hasn't experienced such kindness before.

What a hug; Rebecca said, "My angel; thank you so much,"

Tears in Cal's eyes as he never been so touched.

Disappeared Love   (12/20/20 1:58 a.m.)

We once were so together, but now we've lust apart,

Our love has weakened, broken, where did the betrayal start?

I don't believe you, you kissed me with lies,

Lies like Pinocchio, strings attached, strings that were tied.

I thought you were real, but you were fake like a doll,

I would always see the three dots of your text, but no
message would ever fall.

My steel trust, damaged by your river of tears,

My trust turned to rust, the toxic energy every time you're
near.

Side by side, cuddled on the mattress at rest,

Your lip print to my heart, romantically stamped on my chest.

Sex with you was the reset button for our love,

A melodious cadence of moans echoed to the heavens above.

Something so beautiful and sacred, disappeared from our
vibes,

I was to be your groom, and you were to be my bride.

What a tease life can be, I must be dreaming,

You were my dream, but you disappeared, nightmare
screaming.

You disappeared, where are you, give back my heart,

Rat race world looking for love, beauty always has a head
start.

Perhaps our love has faded,

Perhaps we never should have dated,

Perhaps my hunger for love was too blind, and I ignorantly
ate it.

I left a bite mark in the apple, that was my job, like Steve,

I mean Adam, and you set me up like Eve.

But that's okay, lessons learned,

The bridge has burned,

Ashes to ashes, placed them in a closure urn.

As I say goodbye, may we both disappear from each other's
lives,

Cut the strings attached and be real, be alive.

I don't want to think of you anymore, but of course I will,

My brain has you on file, I have a dream date with you, only
I'm not paying the bill.

Pillows and Covers (12/20/20 2:20 a.m.)

A sleepy head she is, eyes shut for the night,

I sing her a song as she holds my hand firm and tight.

A soft kiss to my middle knuckle,

Another kiss to my hand, I quiver with chills, my heart just buckled.

A handful of her hair, I played with all her curls,

God I'm so lucky to have my baby girl.

I lift the covers to cover her cold shoulders,

I would give the world up to just lay in bed and hold her.

Yet a love so close in spirit is so far in life,

My heart still looks for healing, since she can't be my wife.

I watch as she sleeps, I hope she dreams of me all the way through,

A dream of us dancing and prancing in another planet just for us two,

Oh, she woke up and said, "you should go, it's after 2."

I say, "I missed the last rain, is it okay that I stay?"

An up and down head nod from her, right beside her I lay.

We counted sheep together, she counted hers faster than I counted mines,

In bed with her, feels like I'm frozen in time.

"Just because you have a place for someone in your heart, doesn't mean you'll always have a place for them in your life."

"Life is a circus that hides the popcorn."

Once Upon A Snitch   (12/23/20 8:46 p.m.)

They thought Rube was a friend,

They loved him, ride or die to the end.

Rube had all their trust,

When they went out, he joined, that was a must.

A dark night upon them, up to no good,

They had to make a quick deal in an unfamiliar hood.

Two in the front, Rube's sitting in the back,

Deal or no deal, rules were broken, gunfire attack.

They're driving, bullets flying from out the car,

Enemy went missing, Rube said, "let me out, he couldn't

have gone too far."

Rube hopped out the car and grabbed the piece,

Before he left they said, "make sure his existence cease."

Rube's looking for the enemy, "come out, come out wherever

you are,"

Unbeknownst to him, the enemy was undercover, "freeze,

drop the piece, stand where you are,"

Two cops in the front, now Rube's in the back of a squad car.

Rube's hands are cuffed, read him his Miranda rights,

Complaining to cops, "yo, these cuffs are too tight."

Cops ignored him, took him to the precinct, guilty look in his

mugshot,

Rube had the right to remain silent, but unfortunately, he did not.

A spray of bullets became a spray of words,

They gave Rube fresh beats to his face in the room, then he sung like a bird.

Names, faces, he gave them all of that,

Blue jeans, tattoos, even mentioned the gum stain on the Yankee hat,

Sizes and shapes; one was skinny, and the other was fat.

Real friends grow foe and fake,

Cops caught the other two, saying, "y'all must Rah Rah and Jake?"

A brother they trusted and loved so much,

Shocked at the betrayal, damn he told so much.

Court is in session, Rube pointing his finger saying, "it was them two,"

Rah Rah turned around to see his family, baby mama holding his seed as she just turned two.

Rube pointed to Jake again saying "it was his gun,"

Jake then looked over to his family, devastated to see his crying son.

They never thought he would snitch, not in this lifetime,

Rube runs free while they dropped to their knees as the judge sentenced them for their crime,

Their moms screamed, "NO," as the judge said, "a lifetime."

192

Word Trip

(12/26/20 7:00 p.m.)

Possessions clogged the perception of reality,

Practicality wasted, face it,

Youthful minds cursed with a burst of thirst for drama.

Liars and fires, burning bridges, pornographic desires,

Keeping the minds blind with likes, while love is too

invisible to find.

Running for your lives, husbands cheating on their fake

wives,

Thriving and driving luxurious wheels, shoot to kill, no more

oil as the tea spills.

Greetings through Google meetings,

Zoom in, seeing naked mommas and child beatings.

What is life without your choices,

Political voices saying trust us,

Trust not a soul, too many injustices,

Just in case, cover you face,

Lack of faith to vaccinate,

Looking great, let's do a virtual date,

Masturbating is innovative castrating.

Data getting invaded, privacy faded,

Glass screens and views, mamma I made it.

Blast the screen, now he has to clean,

Oops, too much information, is that Vaseline?

I hate to hate, I know that's too hateful of a word,

But I can't debate, I love to hate, death,

I don't want death, I want all my breath,

Forever and ever, and ever, and ever,

and ever, and ever, and ever, and ever,

Until forever is tired of being forever and

Says "I don't ever want to be forever, ever again."

Charli's Chance

(12/25/20 2:52 p.m.)

It is dawn on a Saturday. A post birthday morning for Charli. A beautiful figure, a tall drink of the freshest water. She had a hell of a late night, a colossal birthday celebration. The big "four-zero" never looked so great on a woman such asCharli. Gorgeous, long brunette hair that twirls all the way down to her back. Full lushes lips that could kiss your darkestday goodbye. Olive-green eyes: she could look into any man'seyes and make him hers for the keeping. She is simply one ofa kind. But as flawless as she comes, she comes alone. She wakes up every morning with a lonely heart. A heart that wasonce broken by a man who she truly believed was her lifelong partner. But he was nothing more but a disappointment, a neglectful disappointment. Coming out of bed, she slid off the covers, stretching the tip-top shape of her five-foot-ten-inch body.

"Hash Brown, where are you baby?" She projected, calling to her cute little Havanese dog.

In he comes into her bedroom, jumping right in her arms. She begins her morning ritual of multiple kisses to his furry face. She named him Hash Brown because of his golden-brown color, the look of a hash brown. As she put Hash Brown down, she walked over to her nightstand and grabbed her phone. Overwhelmed with how many text messages and notifications she received on social media. As she scrolled up the messages sent by her friends, who couldn't make it last night to her rooftop party, Charli began to thank them for the birthday wishes.

"Happy Belated Birthday Charli girly, so sorry I couldn't be there," one of her old friends commented under herFacebook post.

"Aww thank you so much sweetie, it's okay." Charli responded

As Charli looked at the videos of her party, she realized how much fun herself and her friends had, but also how she had one too many drinks last night. But hey, you only turn forty years old once, right?

As Charli was just about finished responding to her birthday wishes, there was one unknown phone number that caught her attention.

"Happy Birthday Charli, it has been a long time. Hope all is well," was the text message sent from the mysterious number.

Sitting on her bed, she looked up from her phone, trying to think who this could possibly be. She text the number back saying, "thank you, but who am I speaking with?"

Charli then tossed her phone on the bed, as she headed to the bathroom, opened the glass door to the shower, and turned on the showerhead. She began to check the temperature of the water, dangling her burgundy nail polished fingers through the lukewarm drops. She then undresses herself out of her birthday outfit, a black mesh dress that shows you the best, and censors the rest. She did not have the chance last night to get undress and put on her pajamas. As I said, she had a hell of a night. The steam from the shower began to fogup the bathroom mirror. A gentle wipe of the misty mirror with her hand, as she looked at her reflection. Charli could not help but think about herself in that moment. Thinking about her life, what she's been through, who she is as a person today, and where she sees herself in the future. Being that Charli is now in her forties, she is officially in the neighborhood of a middle-aged woman.

Even though youth is still reserved on her face, she could actually pass for thirty.

As she was about to hop in the shower, her phone began to ring. A Britney Spears ring tone, from the song "*Baby One More Time*." Charli has been a huge, obsessed fan of Britney Spears since high school, she would even sing that song in the shower. But Charli decided to just let her phone ring while she headed in to rinse off. That running water, spraying all over her body, it did her some good. As she stands in the shower, she could not help but think about the unknown number, and who that person is. She thought about all the people she could think of from her past. But Charli was clueless to who it could be, especially since she changed her phone number several months ago.

As Charli just about finished in the shower, she took the soap and rubbed it on a tattoo she recently had done. The tattoo is a quote that says, "*The Pain Will Win Some Battles, But Love Will Always Win the War*." She discovered this quote in a book she once read, and it stuck with her ever since. Charli had that placed on her left forearm, along with a beautiful red rose. She placed the tattoo over her scars. It was the scars of her self-inflicted cuts.

If I may, allow me to take you into Charli's past for a moment. When Charli was a young teenager, her mother insisted that she sign her up for modeling. She was definitely the girl to do it, she was tall and drop-dead gorgeous. When Charli went to her first open call in New York City, the modeling scouts took that first glance at her, and without question, they signed her on the spot. Charli had a very promising modeling career ahead of her, until she was introduced to the dark side of a model's life, and the darkside of the business. The drinking, the drugs, the much older men, inviting her to have dinner, shopping sprees, and the typical sugar daddy treatment. Men lustfully having their way with her. Charli being just a young, naïve teenage girl, she burnt herself out in a matter of two years.

None of the clientele wanted to work with her anymore, her agency dropped her, and so did her mother. Her mother exiled her from her life, and from her heart. If you could only imagine, a young woman being nineteen years old, and not having her mother in her life, that took a heavy toll on Charli. After Charli's mother abandoned her, Charli made a phone call to her father, asking to live with him until she got herself on her feet. He without hesitation, said yes. Even though she rarely seen her father much of the first nineteen years of her life, Charli was very pleased that she was going to have not only a place to live, but a parent who she loves, and who loves her in return. But the love she received from her father, was not love at all. It was abuse in every way possible. Her father made advances after advances, constantly trying to seduce his own flesh and blood, his own daughter. Until one night, his advances became very intoxicating, predatory, and very violent. That night, he took his advances to the worst level you could ever imagine. He slipped a couple of pills in her water bottle, in no time she passed out, and he did the unthinkable, the unimaginable. He raped Charli, repeatedly.

Many may think, why did Charli stay? Why would she stay with her father, and not get law enforcement involved? Charli's fear, more than ever, was getting her father in trouble, she still held on to the love for her father. But holding on to that love enable her father's abusive nature. She did however call her mother, to let her know what was happening to her. Her mother said maliciously, "I hope he fucks you sideways and throws you in the trash. You embarrass me, you are dead to me."

For a mother to say that to her own daughter, Charli knew that she had no one else to turn to but a father who was just as worse. Her father groomed her, as well as those older men who took advantage of her while she modeled. They brainwashed her into this submissive piece of flesh. Charli feltthat there was nowhere else for her nineteen-year-old self to go. All her modeling income came and went, completely splurged by her greedy, self-centered mother. Charli had nothing to lose, nothing to live for, nothing or no one to love, or to love her. So, one day at her father's house, Charli took a razor, looked at herself in the bathroom mirror and said, "I can't do this anymore. I don't want to be here." Charli then ran down the stairs with the razor, to where her father was in the kitchen. "Hey dad, watch this!" Charli shouted at herfather, while she began to slash herself on her left forearm.

Two of the cuts ran deep, but miraculously missed her arteries. Her father, too little, too late with his guilt. He screamed at Charli saying, "Jesus! STOP!!!" Charli then began to chase her father around the house with the razorblade, eventually making her way out of the house, chasinghim while her arm was bleeding profusely. Charli chased her father around his car, and then out into the middle of the dead-end street. Her father's neighbor came outside of his house to see what all the commotion was about. As the neighbor caught whiff of what was happening, he then tackled Charli to the ground, disarmed her of the razor blade, and told his wife to call the police. The neighbor asked Charli with his fearful voice, "what the hell is going on here?" Charli burst into tears, telling the neighbor, "It's my father, he's been abusing me so badly. I can't live like this anymore."

The neighbor then brought Charli into his house; his wife helped with Charli's bleeding wounds until paramedics arrived. Police were able to track down Charli's father, several blocks away from his house, arrest him, and bring him downto the precinct for booking. As paramedics arrived and placed Charli on the stretcher, Charli could not help but stare at the sky. It was crystal clear, perfect afternoon. She wondered how something as mortifying as this could happen on such a beautiful day? A thousand thoughts swiftly swirling around her mind; her pain, her anger towards her mother, and her sudden feeling of guilt for not leaving. All of this playing a visual dirty mind game on her as she rides inthe ambulance, on her way to the hospital.

That was all Charli could remember about that day, or at least all that she wanted to remember. She has been through a lot. The pain was too great, too powerful to leave those scars naked, constantly reminding her about that horrible time she endured some twenty-one years ago. "I needed this so badly,"Charli said to herself in a soft- spoken tone, with such satisfaction.

As Charli rinsed herself off, she turned off the shower handle, got out of the shower, and grabbed two towels. One towel she wrapped over her hair, and the other over her body.

As Charli walked out of the bathroom, she walked over to her bed to take another look at her phone, to see who gave her that ring, and by ring, I mean call. What she saw on her phone put her in absolute shock. Can you guess who gave her that call? It was her mother. Charli has not spoken to her mother since the last time she called her mother, in the hospital, twenty-one years ago. Charli begged her mother for help when her father was abusing her, and when Charli called her mother in her hospital bed, her mother said this with such conviction, "I'll pray, I'll pray that hospital bed, will soon be your death bed, you slut bitch!" Charli knew, from that point on, that she had no mother.

Being that Charli did not answer the phone, her mother left a voicemail. But the voicemail that Charli's mother left her was even more disturbing than what she said the last time they spoke.

Her mother said with such a demonic spirit, "I didn't call you to wish you a happy birthday. I called to let you know that your father is dead. He killed himself in the same cell that he's been in for the last twenty years, thanks to you, bye. Oh, and by the way, when are you going to kill yourself?" Her mother then hung up.

Can you imagine, not speaking to your mother for over twenty years, and out of the blue, she sends such a soulless voicemail, such as that voicemail? But as for Charli, Charli did not really shed any tears about her father. She was rather relieved to hear the news of his suicide. As far as her mother, she was surprised that her mother called her after two decades but was not surprised at all for such a loathsome remark. However, Charli did want to give her mother a Grade-A piece of retaliation. So, Charli looked at her mother's number and began to give her a call. But then Charli stopped. Charli had to stop and ask herself, "How did she get my new number?" They have not talked in years, how did her mother get a hold of Charli's new number, and let's not forget the mysterious phone number that text Charli and wished her a happy birthday. How did they get her number?

That is when it hit Charli. She placed her new number on her Facebook profile. So clearly, her mother has been snooping around, scoping Charli for quite some time. Charli then decided that it was not worth the exchange of words with her mother. So, she blocked her mother's number, as well as finding her mother's profile on Facebook, and blocking that as well. As far as the mysterious number that text Charli, that unknown person has yet to respond.

In a hurry, Charli began to get dressed, as she realized it was time for Hash Brown's walk. She had on these denim skinny jeans from Hollister, which made her figure look extra curvy. She then put on her favorite burnt orange turtleneck sweater, and yes, she did put on deodorant and lotion. She then slid on her Aldo chocolate-brown Chelsea boots, headed down her stairs, put on her green peacoat and hat, grabbed her keys, and Hash Brown's leash.

"Oh shit," Charli said as she forgot her wallet and phone in her bedroom.

As she ran up her stairs to grab the rest of her things, she grabbed her phone, checked it, and noticed that the mysterious phone number responded. As Charli began to read the text, it brought a much-needed smile to her face. It was a special friend of hers, her friend Jason, who she met some twenty years ago, a little after she was going through all of her troubles with her father.

In the text message, Jason wrote, "You are speaking with Jason, Jason Edwards? We met at a fourth of July barbeque about twenty years ago. I know it has been such a long time, and you probably do not remember me, or even want to talk with me. I just wanted to wish you a Happy Birthday, and you look more beautiful than when the last time I saw you. Oh, in case you are wondering how I have your number, I saw it on your Facebook account, I looked you up and saw your profile. Please add me as a Facebook friend."

Charli took in a deep breath of such happiness. She remembered Jason on that fourth of July day, as if it was yesterday. As Charli was about to stroll down memory lane, she received a round of barks from Hash Brown.

"Okay Hash Brown, momma's coming." Charli said as she ran down the stairs.

Out the door Charli and Hash Brown went as she locked the front entrance to her brownstone home. She then put on her face covering; even though the state gave people the permission to now be mask-free after the outbreak of the COVID-19 pandemic, Charli sometimes still goes out with some caution and stays safe. Plus, she likes how it keeps her face nice and warm.

She did not reply to Jason just yet, she wanted to make him wait a little. Walking down the blanketed sidewalk of autumn leaves with Hash Brown, Charli begins to think about her bittersweet morning. Hearing from her evil, deranged mother, hearing the news about her father's death, and then receiving a text from her special friend, Jason Edwards.

Actually, Jason is the guy who I mentioned earlier, who was the neglectful disappointment. She really had such a special memory with Jason. Charli met Jason back on that fourth of

July day, over twenty years ago. She met Jason through the neighbor, who helped her when she had her breakdown with her father. After Charli recovered, that neighbor took her into his home with his wife and son. He told Charli that she could stay as long as she needed to. They became like her adoptive family; actually, they are her family, and she's been in contact with them ever since.

To give you some backstory, on that fourth of July day, the neighbor's son, Matthew, invited a mutual friend over to the barbeque. That friend was Jason. As Charli was helping Mary, the neighbor's wife, preparing the deviled eggs in the kitchen, there was knock at the door.

"I'll get it," Charli said as she took a big bite out of one of the deviled eggs.

She brushed her hands together, removing the paprika seasoning off of her fingertips before grabbing the doorknob. She opened the door and saw Jason. Her mouth half stuffed with the deviled egg, she looked at him and said, "Hi."

"Hi, I'm Jason, Matt's friend. You must be Charli." He said with his handsomely contagious smile.

Charli still chewing on the deviled egg, she looked at him and just nodded her head up and down with a funny grunt sound. Jason came in with his Pink Floyd "The Dark Side of the Moon" t-shirt, scented with Old Spice deodorant, beige shorts, and white converse. Charli grown to liking him instantly. After letting Jason inside the house, she hurried back to the kitchen to help Mary with the food.

"Oh my God Mary, "I'm freaking drooling right now." Charli said to Mary, as she finished decorating the deviled eggs.

Mary humorously responded to Charli saying, "I knew you would hunny, he is quite the chick magnet, isn't he?"

As Charli started to bring the food out to the back yard, she found it rather difficult to keep her eyes off of Jason, as it was equally difficult for him to keep his eyes off of her. The vibes, the chemistry between the two was a very puissant connection. As all the food was prepared, David, who was the neighbor, Mary's husband, and Matthew's father, he said the grace: "To our father, the holy spirit, we thank you for the wonderful food we are about to receive, we thank you for bringing Charli into our lives, we couldn't be happier to have her in our family. We are also happy to have Jason over to celebrate with us, another Fourth of July of our great country. In Christ name, amen."

As everyone had just about enough to eat, they all went their separate ways around the house. Mary went in the kitchen to wrap up the food, David went in to watch television, sipping on his Jack Daniels, with diet coke on the rocks. Matthew went to the front of the house to take out the trash, as Charli decided to sit in the backyard, with her legs dipped in the beautifully lit pool. Jason was in the backyard as well. The backyard looked like a dream right out of a movie. Little mini pine trees, a deck with lights hanging from above, it was beautiful, and angelic.

"Is it okay if I join you?" Jason asked nervously.

"Sure, come on in, the water is great." Charli said with a splash of flirting gesture.

As Jason took off his Pink Floyd t-shirt, Charli became hypnotized by his chiseled six-pack abs, the most toned body she had ever seen with her own two eyes. Charli was arounda lot of male models for those two years, but never saw such an eloquent, delightful physique such as Jason's. A great splash, as Jason dives in the pool. His swirly underwater imagebegan to swim its way towards Charli's dangling legs. As Jason came to the surface of the water, he slowly approached Charli, almost ruining the moment with an awkward stare.

"I see you keep yourself in shape," Charli said bashfully.

"Yea well, I'm into sports, so I kind of have to keep myself in good shape." Jason said as he blushed.

The two of them began to conversate, laughing and smiling like two teenagers, deep in love, deeper than the pool they were in. The growth of comfort with the two of them instilled confidence in Jason, as he laid his dripping wet head on Charli's left leg, and she began to run her fingers through his silky jet-black hair. As she looked at him, her face began to frown and drift away from his sight.

"Hey, what's wrong?" Jason said as his face was filled with concern.

Charli with reassurance said to him, "nothing, I'm sorry, sometimes I just get caught up in my thoughts, about my past, and my situation with my parents. It's kind of been a rough nineteen years for me."

"Do you want to talk about it? You talk, and I'll listen," Jason said with a sincere open mind.

As soon as Charli was about to speak her mind, there was a bang. Then another, and another, and another. It was fireworks, lighting up the night sky. The both of them turned their heads to look up, seeing the sparks flicker and blossom way up high, staring at an astonishing patriotic vision of amazement. Charli then turned her head to look back at Jason, and Jason looked right back at her.

"Can you swim Charli?" he asked with his trillion-dollar smile.

"Of course, I can swim, I'm like a mermaid." Charli responded with a sense of humor.

"Prove it," Jason said as he picked Charli up from in the pool and had her in his muscular arms.

Charli surprised at his strength, being able to pick up her tall solid body, and then taking her underwater. As the two of them were underwater, looking at each other in a wet and hazy vision, and colorful fireworks lighting up the entire pool. It was like a visual masterpiece right out of a Disney movie. At that very intimate moment, Charli and Jason shared their first and unforgettable kiss, deep underwater. It was like beingin a world that only they knew of; no disturbance, just the twoof them. It was like time stood still for them. Every time they kissed; another firework exploded. It was the look of a dream into a deep blue romantic abyss. It couldn't have been a more perfect moment. As the shortness of breath began to affect the moment, they both came back up to the surface of the pool, gasping for oxygen, but that didn't stop the continuous locking of lips with each other. Kiss after passionate kiss, they couldn't resist themselves. As Jason began to kiss underneathCharli's cleft chin, she tilted her head up to the sky, and saw those beautiful fireworks. She felt like she was on cloud 9, like the two of them were floating around in the fireworks, dancing and kissing the night away, surrounded by fiery sprinkles of paradise. She didn't want it to stop.

"Um, do you guys need a room or something?" Matthew said, interrupting their special moment.

"Oh, fuck," Charli blurted out loud.

"I guess I'll leave you guys be for a little while. Nice fireworks, huh?" Matthew said as he walked back into the house.

As for Jason and Charli, their momentous connection reached its destination. They both began to drift away from each other in the pool, Jason drifting off to one side, while Charli drifted off to the other. They said not one word to each other, yet they locked eyes. Jason then turned around to grab the side of the wall, leaped up and out of the pool. He then dried off, and just walked away. Perhaps the moment was so real, so divine, that Charli and Jason had no words for it. As Charli got out of the pool, she went into the bathroom, took a deep breath, and exhaled while she looked at herself in the mirror. It wasn't until then, she realized that she felt true love, for the very first time in her life. Her father was an absolute predator to her, as well the decrepit old men she encountered in the fashion world, who treated her like an object of no importance. But with Jason, she didn't feel any of

212

that. For the very first time, she was treated and respected asa woman, and as a human being. As she got herself together and came out of the bathroom, she walked around to look for Jason. But he was nowhere in sight, absolutely nowhere.

"Hey Matt, did you see where Jason went?" Charli asked with eager concern.

"Oh, I think he went home. It's funny, I thought he was coming back, because he left with no shirt on." Matthew said with a few chuckles

Charli was appalled, even a little heartbroken that he would just up and leave, especially without saying goodbye. She didn't want anyone to see her cry, so she moved swiftly to the backyard, and immediately let it all out. She cried enough tears to make a pool of her own. As Charli cried her eyes out in the backyard, she notices Jason's Pink Floyd shirt hanging off of the chair. She walked over to the chair, grabbed the shirt, and began to smell it. The echo of scent from his Old Spice deodorant was all over the shirt. She placed his shirt over her face, covering her face completely, and began to cry some more. She cried and cried as the aftermath of fireworks began to spark the sky for the remainder of the night. That was the last time she ever saw him.

As of today, over twenty years later, it is still an unforgettable, romantic mystery. Charli was left with many questions that needed answers. As Charli just about finished up with walking Hash Brown, she goes to grab a coffee from the local coffee shop to get her usual. A Pumpkin Spice flavored coffee with extra cream always hits the spot for her.

"Hey Sarah, good morning, I'll have the usual." Charli said to Sarah the cashier.

"Heyyy, not a problem, I'll have that for you. Hi Hash Brown," Sarah said with enthusiasm.

In no time, Charli's coffee was ready; she grabbed it, paid with Apple Pay, and waved goodbye. Charli was a little anxious to head back home. She wanted to talk with Jason as soon as possible. She had a few blocks to go before arriving home. Every step of the way, all she could do was think about him. She was going back and forth with her feelings. She didn't know if she should be happy that he got in contact withher, after all these years, or angry for leaving her under such astray circumstances. Mixed feelings dancing in her Libra mind. As she finally made her way inside her house, she unhooked Hash Brown off his leash, and he went running overto chew away on his favorite bacon-flavored bone. She then placed her keys and coffee on her kitchen table, took off her hat and peacoat, placed it in her closet, kicked off her Chelsea boots, pulled out her phone, and began to respond to Jason's text.

Charli really wanted the answers from his own mouth, she didn't want the answers revealed via text message. So, she responded to Jason saying, "Omg, Jason? Yes, it has been a very long time. Listen, do you think we could talk over the phone? I would prefer that actually." She sent that text to him, as she began to sip on her coffee, waiting for him to reply.

As she waited, she continued to sip her coffee, laying on her living room couch, tapping her fingers at the bottom of her coffee cup. She then looked over at Hash Brown, who was still chewing on his bone. Her patience started to weaken, as Jason's response is nowhere in sight on her phone. Then she received a notification, she flipped her phone over so fast to look at the screen.

"Happy Belated Birthday Charli! I wish you many more," A text sent by one of her co-workers.

"Thank you, Tomi," Charli responded with gratitude, butwith weak enthusiasm, as she waits for Jason's response.

The clock continued to tick away, the sun was on its way down the horizon, and Jason has yet to respond. The long waiting drained Charli for the day. She took the last sip of her coffee thirty minutes ago, and she didn't have enough energy left to stay awake. Her heavy eyes began to shut as she fell asleep on her very comfy couch. As she slept, her body began to jerk and twitch with grunting noises, as she was having herself a nightmare. A nightmare of the abuse she suffered from at the hands of her father, those dirty old men, as well as the abuse she survived by the hands of her ex-boyfriend, who she met after meeting Jason. It was flashback moments of them hitting her, kicking her whileshe was on the ground. In her nightmare, she was pleading with all of them saying, "stop, stop please! I can't breathe, you're hurting me." She kept seeing herself cut her arm in the nightmare, over and over. Tossing and turning, and then a scream emerged through the REM of her sleep.

Finally, she snapped out of the nightmare and woke up. Heavy breathing with a deep sweat, as she looks around her now dark living room. She quickly switched on her alabaster white lamp and called for Hash Brown.

"Hash Brown, Hash Brown!" Charli shouted.

Hash Brown then made his way down the stairs, as she could hear his new bell collar that she bought him when they went out earlier. He hopped up on the couch with Charli and began to lick away at her sweaty face.

"Hey, stop that," Charli said to Hash Brown with a calm giggle.

As she put Hash Brown on the floor, Charli took a look at her phone, and she finally received a text from Jason. At first it gave her a little anxiety to see it, and a minor dopamine release.

As she read the text, Jason typed, "Better yet, can we actually meet in person? I see that you live in the city, I figured maybe we can meet up, and have a drink? Dinner perhaps, if I'm not pushing it?"

"I would like that actually. Yes, can you meet me at DeLiano's Restaurant, let's say at 8:30 p.m.?" Charli responded to Jason.

Jason came right back with a response. From the look of her smiling face, she had a date for the night. But she had no time to waste, as it was already 6:05 p.m. It takes her a long time to get ready. So, she got up from her couch, ran up her stairs, and got the shower running. She then went into her closet and had absolutely no idea of what to wear. It's been over twenty years since they last saw each other. They were practically young kids when they met for the first and only time. Charli didn't know whether she should wear something sexy, something casual, or very casual. She thought to herself, "wait a minute, what if he's married with kids or something?" But after a few minutes of thinking it over, she went with her gut and wanted to make a very good impression. She wanted Jason to know that after twenty years, she still got it.

She found just the right dress for this very special occasion. She decided on this very eloquent, all black dress, with a strap that wraps around her neck, and a very exotic design in the front, that reveals just enough cleavage, to where it is "classy, but not trashy." She then laid the dress on her bed and headed in for a quick shower. After she got out of the shower, she then wiped the mist off of her mirror, just as she did earlier that morning, and looked at her reflection. In her mind, she felt that this would be her chance, her second chance at redemption. What she felt and experienced with Jason, some twenty-years ago, was the most picturesque, undeniably romantic chapter of her life. A chapter of unfinished business, unanswered questions at the tip of her tongue. She is ready for this; she's been ready for a very long time.

The vintage clock hanging in her bedroom displays the time of 7:51 p.m. As she is just about finished with her hair and makeup, she received another text from Jason.

"Hey, I am just getting into the city now, I should be at Deli Anos Restaurant at around 8:15 ish?" Jason's text to Charli.

Charli responded humorously, "It's called "DeLiano's" Restaurant, LOL. And okay, I should be there around the same time. See you soon."

"Autocorrect, LOL." Jason responding to Charli's text.

The closer it got to the time, the more excited and nervous Charli became. Her hair was ready, her makeup was ready, she was ready, and her Uber driver was on his way. She was ready to take on this night of pure mystery. All she had left to do was put on her red bottom shoes, grab her faux fur coat, and head on out the door. But before she went, she poured a little cup of doggie treats in Hash Brown's bowl, withsome fresh water in his other bowl.

She then picked Hash Brown up and said, "you be a good boy okay? Momma's going out to catch up with an old friend. More like a long-lost lover. Wish me good luck."

She kissed Hash Brown and put him down. He then walked over to feast on his treats. Fully dressed as she grabbed her phone and keys and locked up. Her Uber was right on time, as well as she will be, as the time was 8:07 p.m., and lived only five blocks away from DeLiano's. As she's riding in her Uber, her palms began to accumulate a clammy sensation. Her nerves were getting to her, because she was so excited. Excited to possibly relived what she's been missing from her life, for so long. Finally, the Uber makes its way in front of DeLiano's Restaurant.

"Thank you, have a good night," Charli said to her Uber driver.

"You're welcome sweetheart. Oh, by the way, whoever your date is, tell him he's a lucky man, and he better not screw it up." Said her Uber driver.

"Thanks, I hope he doesn't screw it up either." Charli responded with a light chuckle.

As she got out, she checked her phone to make sure Jason didn't text her saying he's here. She didn't want to go in the restaurant without him. So, she decided to wait outside for him. About five minutes goes by, still no sign of him. Charli then text him saying, "hey, just wanted to let you knowI'm outside waiting for you. I don't want to go in without you." She continues to wait, as the chilly strong breeze flowsthrough the magnificent curls of her hair. She began to look up at the sky, seeing the stars, reminiscing about the first timeher and Jason met, their first kiss, and now it's finally going tohappen again.

As she waits outside, a car pulls up in front of DeLiano's, an all-black Bentley with tinted windows. As she looks at the car, her phone began to ring. It was Jason calling her. As she answered her phone and looked up, she saw a man coming out of the back seat of the Bentley, on his phone, soon to figure out it was Jason.

"I see you, I'm…I'm over here," Charli said to Jason over the phone.

"Where?—Oh, I see you now." Jason said and then hung up his phone.

My God, if only you could see their faces when they looked at each other. It was like they were seeing each other again, just like the first time when Charli opened the door, her mouth stuffed with the deviled egg, and he just stared right back at her. Charli started to walk towards him, and he began to walk towards her. They met halfway in front of the DeLiano's main entrance. Not many words were exchanged just yet; just embracing each other. Jason, dressed in an all-black Tom Ford suit, with a classy turtleneck sweater, and black leather loafers. He's still as handsome as she could ever imagine, with a few gray hairs in his neatly groomed beard. He then reached out his hand for her to hold. She looked down at his hand, happy and so relieved to find no wedding ring in sight, no sign of him being betrothed. She placed her hand on top of his; he gently, oh so gently pulled her towards him, and her body gracefully collided with his for the longest minute. She closed her eyes as tears began to leak their way out down her face. He even still had the same Old Spice scent that she smelt on his Pink Floyd t-shirt, that night he left it near the pool.

"I've waited so long for this, I thought I'd never see you again." He said as he lifted Charli's head up and looked at her.

"God, you're going to make me mess up my makeup." Charli responded with an ice breaker

They both broke into laughter, a wise move by Charli. They finally made their way into DeLiano's Restaurant. Beautiful place, amazing pieces of artwork around the walls. Pictures of world-famous celebrities from the good ole days. A very nice, dimed look, with just enough light to see your meals.

Charli could not take her eyes off of him. It was like twenty years didn't even go by for these two, they picked up right where they started, except this time, they are dry.

"Good evening, do you have reservations?" The host said to Charli.

"Good evening, and yes we do, I made reservations for Charli and Jason." Charli said to the host.

"Perfect, great! Right this way please." The host said as she escorted them to their reserved table.

They both took their seats; Charli immediately grabbed the napkin from out of her glass to wipe her eyes from all the tears. As she looked up to see Jason, he was looking right back at her, with his trillion-dollar smile. It was as if they were those two teenagers who fell in love again. But Jason knew he had a lot of explaining to do. So, he didn't waste any time.

"I take it that you have some questions for me, and rightfully so." Jason said to Charli with a tone of guilt.

Charli responded rather with hesitation, "well, yes I do. It was very difficult for me to understand why you just up and left without saying a word to me."

Jason began to look down at his empty reserved dinner plate, then he took a sip of the DeLiano's red wine special, thinking of what he needs to say to Charli. As he held his glass up near his face, he takes another sip and looks at Charli with this peccable look of error. He knew the truth was the only way he could ever redeem himself. He knew after all these years, that Charli deserved to know the truth about him, and why he left her in such a shady fashion.

"Well Charli," said Jason. "You deserve to know the truth, and here it is—"

"Wait, are you gay? Because that could explain it entirely." Charli asked as she interrupted Jason.

"Woah, oh my God, no! That's very postulating of you to ask me that." Jason responded with the quickness,

"I'm sorry, I just wanted to surprise you I guess." Charli said with a little embarrassment.

Jason then gathered his thoughts and words together, and finally said to Charli, "That night when we kissed underwater, it was like we were in a dream together, except it was very much real. I never experienced something like that in my entire life. Not before, nor did I feel it afterwards. But when I felt it with you, I was not entirely available to be doing something like that with another woman. I was in a relationship when I first met you. I was together with my girlfriend for three years prior to when you opened the door, and I laid my eyes on you for the very first time. It was pure magic, what I felt when I first saw you. I never felt that connection from anyone else like that before. Not from my girlfriend at the time, or no other woman ever since. But I felt so guilty, I felt so wrong for stepping out, cheating on my girlfriend, and I didn't want you getting involve in my betrayal,and to create a mess. I just had no words for you at that time. So, I got out of the pool, without saying a word, and I left. I went back to see my girlfriend that same night, and I knew, at that very moment, we were not going to last. I knew after ourmoment in the pool, I was never going to have that with her. I

224

was so young, and so stupid. I just want you to know Charli, I am so sorry, I hope you find it in your heart to one day forgive me, and maybe, just maybe, we could give this another chance?"

A lot for Charli to sink in right now. She felt that he answered some of her questions, but there is still something that she feels he is keeping from her. Just as Charli begins to open her mouth to speak to Jason, the waiter makes his way to their table.

"Hi folks, good evening, I'm Louie, I'll be your waiter for tonight, I see you have your wine already, that's great. Can I start you off with an appetizer or are you ready to order the entrées?" The waiter said so perfectly in his Italian accent.

"Oh, ladies first," Jason said respectfully.

"Thank you, I'll just have your special, the lobster and spinach quiche please," Charli said to the waiter.

"Oh, that is a very good choice, it is one of our highest demands. And for you sir?" Louie the waiter responded.

"You know that sounds absolutely delicious, I think I'll have that as well." Jason said as he looked over to Charli.

Louie the waiter then collected both of their menus and walked off with their orders. Charli was really at a loss for words after Jason broke it down for her. She began to take a few sips of red wine herself. As she placed her glass on the table, Jason couldn't help but glance at the red lip print Charli left on the rim of her glass. Then, a brief moment of awkward silence. Twenty years apart from each other can't be easy.

"I'll be right back, I'm going to use the restroom," Charli said to Jason.

"Oh, okay, take your time," Jason responded as he takes another sip of wine.

As Charli headed to the restroom, her thoughts about what she wants to ask Jason were blurry and unclear. She doesn't want to ask him such personal questions, with the potential of stepping on his toes in the process. She doesn't want to get too personal and possibly ruin this special moment. As she makes her way into the ladies' room, she begins to pace herself, walking back and forth in her high heeled red bottoms. Giving herself some time to breathe and calm down. She then looks at herself in the mirror. As she looks, she doesn't say a word, just deep in her thoughts. Thinking of what she is deciding to ask and tell him. She has some skeletons in the closet, unbeknownst to him, just as much as he may have.

As Charli stood there in front of the mirror, another woman came into the restroom. A woman who looked to be in her sixties, yet she was dressed to kill. She had on a white Alexander Wang dress, with a suspended fishline, a pearl necklace with the matching earrings, and a diamond bracelet; she looked absolutely amazing. The older woman had this short blonde hair style, a Jane Fonda look so to speak, with a very classy persona. Charli quickly turned on the facet to wash her hands, to make it seem like she was doing something besides just staring at the mirror. The older woman walked over, right beside Charli, to do a touchup of her lipstick and powdered her nose a bit. As Charli couldn't help herself, she shed a tear or two, and the older woman caught notice to it.

"Darling, are you okay?" The older woman asked Charli.

"I don't know, I'm in such limbo here." Charli said emotionally to the older woman.

"What's the problem my dear? Tell me, I've been around for quite some time now. It's about a man, isn't it?" The older woman asked Charli.

Charli responded as she wiped her tears away, "Yes, yes, it is about a man. I haven't seen him in over twenty years, and all of a sudden, he just comes back into my life. He's right out there, sitting at the table, and I don't know how to feel about this. I'm excited, I'm nervous, I'm just all over the place. I only met him once prior to tonight, twenty years ago, and he left me without a word. I was so heartbroken, but I… I'm still in love with him. Ma'am, does this all sound crazy?"

"Oh God my dear, please don't call me ma'am. I'm already certified as a senior citizen; I do not want that old woman stamp on me just yet. Call me Camella." The older woman said to Charli with an original sense of humor.

"Oh, sorry, it's nice to meet you Camella, I'm Charli." Charli said to Camella as she shook her hand.

Camella then said to Charli, "Baby, I've been in love with so many men in my life. More than I can remember. Some lied to me, cheated on me, and…even put their hands onme. I've been through it all. Hell, I've even survived cancer. Yet no matter what, I kept moving forward. I never let the hardtimes stop me from living. I'm too alive to stop living. Yes, life can be so wrong, so unfair, yet it can also be so beautiful. If only you stop to look at it in the moment of now. You cannotchange the past. All you can do is learn from it and keep moving forward. I said this in one of my books, "The Pain Will Win Some Battles, But Love Will Always Win the War."

Charli's face dropped with disbelief. She realized then that her favorite quote that she tattooed on her left arm, was written by this older woman that she is actually talking with at this very moment. The older woman is critically acclaimed author, the one and only, "Camella Deltona."

"Oh my God, I didn't recognize you, or the fact that you are the author of the book, "*You're Too Alive*." I have that very same quote tattooed on my arm. See?" Charli said as she showed her arm to Camella.

"Oh my lord, darling I'm so deeply flattered and honored, but did that hurt?" Camella asked Charli with a concerned look on her face.

"Oh, not at all," Charli responded. "I got this tattoo to cover up a few scars that I didn't want to be reminded of anymore. You have no idea how much your book helped me;your words changed my life."

After hearing that, a few tears even fell down from the eyes of Camella. She really was not expecting such a shocking moment of fate. Camella was overly pleased that someone took to her work so much, that they would even make a permanent marking of her words on their body. Camella had to get herself together before she headed back out to her table.

"Ah Girly, what a sweet gesture, I'm actually getting choked up right now." Camella said to Charli with a wave of emotion.

"You have inspired me so much with your words Ms. Deltona. You gave me a reason to leave the pain in the past." Charli said as she caves into her emotions as well.

"Oh please, call me Camella. Good lord, now I have to redo my eyeliner. You see what you've done?" Camella said humorously to Charli.

"I know, I'm sorry. But what were the odds of this? I just had this tattoo done three weeks ago, and now here you are,I actually meet you in person." Charli said with such satisfaction.

Camella then quickly fixed her eyeliner. As she looked in the mirror, she said to Charli, "And that's life darling, you never know what it will throw at you. All you can do is enjoy it, to the fullest, leave the past in the past, and keep on keeping on, with no regrets. Also, when you know it's true, don't keep love waiting. True love comes with two factors: it only comes once in a lifetime, and it comes with imperfections. If your true love is out there waiting for you at that table, rekindle it, and watch the fireworks fly."

It was as if Charli met her fairy Godmother. Camella gave her all the advice she needed, in just a short period of time. Charli was forever grateful.

"And now, I have to go. It was lovely to meet you Charli, and thank you for your acknowledgement of my work,via a tattoo. Best of luck darling." Camella said as she bids farewell to Charli with a kiss on each cheek.

230

"Uh, hold on, I got some lipstick on you," Camella said as
he rubbed the print of her lipstick off of Charli's cheek.

"Thank you, Camella, take care," Charli said as
Camella walked out of the restroom.

Right before Charli made her way out of the ladies'
room, she took one last look in the mirror, this time with a smile
on her face. She was ready, ready to walk back out there, face
her fears and doubts, and take a chance at love again, even if it is
not perfect. As Charli came out of the ladies' room, she stood
behind one of the marble pillars, hiding herself from Jason, and
looking at him from a distance. As she looked, the lobster
and spinach quiche had arrived at their table. Charli noticed
that Jason did not touch his food yet. She realized then that he
wouldn't start until she came back to the table. Perhaps
chivalry is still very much alive. But Charli knew Jason's
patience was thinning as he began to look at his watch and look
around, wondering where she was.

"Is there something you need madam?" Louie the waiter
standing behind Charli.

"Oh, um… No, I'm fine, thank you," Charli said as she heads
back to the table.

"Hey, there you are. You had me a little worried there. I thought you walked out on me or something." Jason said to Charli with a harmless grin.

Charli responded, "Oh no, of course not, and sorry to keep you waiting. So, shall we begin with this DeLiano's special?"

The two of them began to talk as they enjoyed their meal together, smiling and laughing with such enthralling chemistry. They went on and on; Jason told her about how he started his own Hedge fund company almost a decade ago, as well as real estate development. He traveled all over the world; London, Rome, Hong Kong, Tokyo, Paris, you name it, he's been there. Things changed drastically when the pandemic hit, so he had to cancel many of his trips. Charli was amazed at how well he was doing for himself, and how he still stayed in contact with Matthew over the years.

A little hesitant she became when it was time to share a little bit about herself. She kept it pretty basic and brief with Jason. She told him about how she lived with Matt, Mary and David when things were growing more dysfunctional with her parents. She talked about how she became a very successful buyer for a fashion showroom, as well as a mentor at a non-for-profit organization, that helps young woman who went through specific troubles in life. But she didn't tell Jason the whole truth about her, at least not yet. But ironically, he didn't tell her his whole truth either.

"Charli, you know there is something that I have not mentioned to you, that I think is actually very important for you to know about." Jason said as he finished his last bite of the lobster and spinach quiche.

As soon as he said that, Charli pressed her lips together, with steam coming from out her nose, hypothetically speaking. She had a feeling that he had something else rolled up his sleeves. But after having that brief talk with Camella in the ladies' room, she reminded herself that she is not in control, nor can she change the past. So whatever Jason had to say, it was simply one of those imperfections that her and Camella talked about.

"Lay it on me Jay," Charli said to Jason with mental preparation.

"Okay, so I...I have a kid, a daughter. Her name is Bobbi." Jason said to Charli.

"Oh, wow. That's news. And how old is Bobbi?" Charli asked Jason.

"She just had a birthday about several days ago. She turned fourteen. Her birthday's on the 11th. She's my favorite Libra.

"Really? I just celebrated my birthday yesterday." Charli said with a surprised reaction.

"Isn't that something, what are the odds of that?" Jason responded.
"Yes, only four days apart. And you had Bobbi with the same girlfriend from the time we met?" Charli asked Jason.

Jason responded, "No, it was with someone else, my ex-fiancée. My girlfriend that I told you about, we broke it off six months after you and I met. Some years after that, I met my fiancée at the time, and got her pregnant rather quickly than we planned. Then after we had Bobbi, we both realized that we were not made for each other. So, we didn't even bother to move forward with anything. But we do very well with co-parenting."

It was a lot to unwind for Charli, a man she had fallen in love with over twenty years ago, he's a father to another woman's child. All she could think of is the word "imperfections." She understood that twenty years is a long time. Life goes on, and people go on with their lives. Maybe her selfish tendencies got the best of her, and now she can humble herself, and just carry on with the rest of the night and see where things go.

"So, do *you* have any littles ones running around the house?" Jason humorously asked Charli.

Charli laughed and said, "Well, as a matter a fact I do have a little one running around my house, possibly right now as we speak. My little Hash Brown."

"Hash Brown?" Jason asked with a brief chuckle.

"Yea, he's my Havanese dog. I love him to death, he's my best friend. He keeps me company every day," Charli responded.

"How is everything going? Would you like anything else? Dessert perhaps?" Louie the waiter asked Charli andJason.

"I think we're good Louie, thank you. I'll take the bill." Jason said to Louie the waiter.

As the night was young, Jason and Charli still had some more to catch up on. Jason had this idea of him and Charli taking a ride out in the city, only his vision was not to take a ride in an Uber or a cab. Jason had something much more romantic in mind. As Jason received the dinner bill and wrote his signature on the merchant copy of his receipt, he looked up and said this to Charli,

"You know, it is a perfect night to take a ride out in the city. How about we take a ride through Central Park, on a Horse and Carriage?"

With a smile of romantic approval, Charli said, "I'd love that very much. You know, all these years of living in New York, I've actually never done that."

Jason's plan for the two of them was set. He made reservations for the horse and carriage on his phone. As they grabbed their belongings, Jason took a quick trip to the restroom. Charli told him she will just wait for him at the door. As she waited, she thought about the reason why she never took a ride on a horse and carriage. Her reason was very understandable, as she absolutely hated the smell of horses, unquestionably. The fact that they were going to actually ride behind two horses, and potentially smelling them, she was hoping he might change his mind at the last minute. But then again, Charli wouldn't miss this moment with Jason for the world. She was willing to make this night as perfect as it can be, in an imperfect world.

As Charli waited near the front entrance, she to a look behind her. Looking back at the tables, she saw Camella sitting down with her entourage, laughing and having a terrific time. In that exact moment, Camella turned and saw Charli standing at the door. Charli waved at Camella and

Camella then winked her eye, blew a kiss at Charli, and waved goodbye. That warmed Charli's heart so much.

"Okay, you're all set?" Jason asked Charli as he made his way over from the restroom.

"Yes, I'm good to go. Charli responded.

Being that they were so close to the west side of Central Park, they walked over to where the reserved horse and carriage was located. Charli standing close to six feet, two inches in her heels, was quite satisfied with Jason's six-foot, three- inch frame. She loved the fact that he was still taller than her, even while she wore her favorite heels. They held each other's hands the whole time they walked. Jason began to tell Charli about Bobbi, and how she's really into makeup and cosmetics, also her obsession with TikTok.

"I just don't get it; all she wants to do is create these videos on her social media. I mean don't get me wrong, she's one smart cookie, but come on." Said Jason, as he went on a rant.

"Oh, well she's young, she may get bored of those things eventually, and grow out of it." Charli said, as she wrapped her arm around Jason's arm, and placed her head on his shoulder.

After seven minutes of walking, Charli and Jason made their way over to the Central Park horse and carriage rental. They met with the coachman who was taking them on their romantic ride through Central Park. As Charli stood next to the carriage, she already began to grow irritated by the smell of the horses. But she did not want to ruin the moment. She dealt with it like a champ.

"Ladies first," Jason said to Charli as he gave her a hand and helped her up on the carriage.

"Are you lovely couple all set to go?" The coachman said to Charli and Jason."

"Yes sir, take us away." Jason responded.

Even though Charli was not a fan of the horses' hygiene, she was very much in love with the way they looked. Two of the most beautifully black Clydesdale horses she had ever seen. Their long shiny black hair, with the white hair coveringtheir colossal hooves. The look of the horses outmatched theirsmell, ten to zero for Charli.

As they ride through the park, Charli and Jason did not really say much to each other. Jason just had his arm around Charli's shoulders, giving her that comfort, and she most definitely appreciated it. Clicking after clicking, the horses clicking feet as they were halfway finished with the ride, Charli had a moment, within that moment. An epiphany so to speak. She realized then, after all this time, Jason did not once ask her about what happened to her before they met. He didn't ask about her relationship with her father or her mother. She thought that perhaps he didn't really care about all of that, or maybe he didn't want to step on her toes.

As Charli then looked around at the multi-colorful Central Park trees, she looked at Jason and said to herself at that moment, she wasn't going to tell him about her tormented past. She wasn't going to tell him how her mother was a heartless, evil bitch to her, who was jealous of her own daughter, ever since she was thirteen years old. Charli's mother was always jealous of her looks; the more beautiful Charli became, the more jealous her mother grew of her. As far as her father, and what he did to her; Charli thought about it and said to herself, "he's dead now, I will never have to worry about that monster again." After the news of her father's suicide that morning, Charli's heart gain permanent closure.

But the truth is, for Charli, this was her chance to actually have true love. Charli strongly felt that if she were to tell Jason about what happened to her, something that happened twenty years ago, that it would ruin her true love with Jason, and instead, the only love he would be willing to offer her is "pity love." If Charli told Jason how her father raped her, or how her mother was no mother at all, her fear is that his perception of her would change, and his love for her would be more compelling, than actually it being true. And Charli couldn't accept that.

Her past is now a secret that she will take to her grave. Even though she has nightmares of her past, as she did earlier in the afternoon, Charli can now leave it in the past. Her mother is out of her life, once and for all, her father is now dead, and so is her past.

As Jason and Charli reached the destination of their horse and carriage ride, Jason reached in his wallet, gave the coachman a very nice tip, and they both went on their way. The evening was just about to come close to the finish line of midnight, so Jason decided to walk with Charli to her house, which was not so far away from where the coachman dropped them off. As they walked, Jason went on to talk about his company, and how real estate is beginning to pick up again. He told Charli about his brand-new house in New Jersey, builtfrom scratch. He pulled out his phone from his coat pocket and showed her pictures of the house.

"Oh my God, that is absolutely gorgeous, you designed this?" Charli asked with enthusiasm.

"Well, I had some help, a lot of help actually. But it was worth the wait." Jason said to Charli.

240

As they make their way in front of the stoop to Charli's brownstone, Jason received a call. It was his daughter, Bobbi.

"Excuse me one second Charli, it's Bobbi." Jason said as he answered his phone.

"Oh, it's okay. Actually, just come on up, come inside." Charli said to Jason, as she led the way.

As Charli began to walk up the stairs of herbrownstone, she knew that once Jason came inside, she would not want him to leave. As she turned the key to unlock her door, she was welcomed in with a bunch of barks from Hash Brown.

"What are you still doing up, huh?" Charli said as she picked him up, and he began to lick her face.

Charli then introduced Hash Brown to Jason, who was still on the phone with his daughter Bobbi. In one hand, Jason is holding his phone, and with the other, he shook Hash Brown's paw.

"You must be Hash Brown, it's nice to meet you my furry friend," Jason whispered while covering the speaker to his phone.

As Charli put Hash Brown down, she said to Jason, "Um, you can have a seat, and make yourself at home. I'm just going to change out of this dress really quick, I smell like the damn horses. " Jason said while covering his phone again, "Oh, okay no problem, take your time."

Charli then one by one removed her red bottom high heeled shoes from her feet, as well as took off her faux fur coat, and placed them in her coat closet. She then ran up her stairs, with Hash Brown following behind her. As she got to her bedroom, she loosened up the strap of the dress from around her neck, and the dress went straight down to her ankles. Before she went back downstairs, Charli wanted to somehow present herself as being seductive towards Jason. She didn't know whether or not she should just be in the nude but be covered in her bathrobe, or wear her bra and panties, and then put on her bathrobe. She really didn't want to come off as trashy with her true love, so she chose the second approach.

"Hey Jason, I'll be right down. Are you okay?" Charli shouted down from the top of the stairs. Jason responded, "Oh yea, I'm fine, take your time. That was my daughter Bobbi. She just had to tell me about her TikTok video, and how it received over a hundred thousand views, or likes or whatever those things reward you with.

"Woah, that's actually not bad at all." Charli responded as she was a bit impressed.

Charli finally freshened up, removed her makeup, tied her hair up into a messy bun, hung her horse smelling dress back in her closet, and slid on her furry slippers. As she took a look at herself in the mirror, she looked over to Hash Brown, who was laying there in his comfy, cherry red sofa bed, and she said, "momma's going to need some privacy tonight baby, I'll put your bed downstairs."

So, that's what she did. Charli grabbed Hash Brown's sofa bed, brought it downstairs, and placed it in the Hallway. As she made her way to the living room, where Jason was sitting, she asked him if he wanted something to drink, but he didn't. In fact, all he really wanted at that moment was for Charli to sit with him. He gently patted his hand on the cushion of the couch, a simple gesture of wanting Charli to sit right next to him. But Charli did even better than that, as she saton Jason's lap.

All five-ten of her sexiness, wrapped up in her bathrobe, is now being held by the man of her dreams. She began to gently run her fingers through his hair, as he caresses the smooth blanket of skin, covering her flawless body. It didn't take long for the power of her seduction to pull him in. The two of them, looking each other in the eyes, and after twenty-one years of disconnect, the magic was still there. And then, it was the moment they both have been waiting for the whole night; their second kiss. Kiss after kiss was given, they couldn't stop, they couldn't keep their hands off of each other. Charli repositioning her body to sit on top of Jason, as Jason gently untangled the waist strap from Charli's bathrobe.

Jason took a moment to observe her half-naked body. He then took a firm grip of her curvaceous hips, lifted her up as she wrapped her legs around his waist. They began spinning around several times, as he then had her up against the wall, next to the stairs. He then took off his suit jacket, as Charli began to unbutton his pants. The staircase began to be decorated by Jason's clothes, as they passionately kissed their way up the stairs. As both of them were down to their underwear at the top of the stairs, Charli then back peddled her way into the bedroom, pulling Jason in with her. No disturbance as Hash Brown is downstairs dreaming the night away. No phone calls, no strings attached, just those same two teenagers who fell in love, finishing what they started twenty-one years ago.

As they kiss, Jason lifted Charli up again, and tossed her on the bed. As Charli observed Jason's physique, she realized that he really hasn't missed a day in the gym. The same rock-solid six pack abs she was rubbing on in the pool, on that fourth of July night. As they got more into the depths of fornication, Charli took her softly pedicured feet and pressed them onto Jason's firm, semi-hairy chest. Jason was all for the kinkiness, as he took Charli's right foot, and began to kiss all over it. Kissing the arch of her sole, the balls of her foot, and then the sudden urge of sucking her toes. "Oh *my*, this is a first for me. I'm actually loving it, please proceed." Charli said as her and Jason broke into a moment of laughter.

As Charli took away her right foot, she then presented Jason with her left foot saying, "my left foot is now jealous." Jason then performed the same sticky podiatric routine. As he made his way pass her ankle, up her legs, he began kissing his way up to her stomach, and landing his face in the cleavage of her covered bosom. Charli reached behind her, to unhook her bra, and then Jason went to town.

A magical night for these two. Both naked, like adult newborns, passionate love making, sexual positions they've never endured before, Charli being kissed in places she's never felt. As she gets on top of Jason, he kissed her on the same place that he kissed her in the pool. He kissed her right underneath her cleft chin. She remembered it like it was yesterday, when she tilted her head up, looking at the sky, and the fireworks were live. His tongue making its way all on her neck, kissing and biting her chin, and then making his way back to her lips. His moans began to grow, while her moans grew louder. The sweating, the biting, the smacking of each other's bottoms, and with all the noise they were making, they didn't need any fireworks that night.

It was time for the two of them to catch their breaths, as they concluded their third round of sweaty orgasms. As they lay in bed, under the silky sheets, Charli laid her head on Jason's chest. He plays with her long damped brunette hair, while she rubs her fingers on the curly hairs of his chest. Charli looked at the vintage clock on her wall, saw that the time was 2:13 a.m. As Charli was completely satisfied with her delightful evening, she couldn't help but think about the first time she met Jason. When they first met and had their first kiss, he disappeared. She began to worry herself, thinking what if she wakes up in the morning, and he's gone. Out of her life once again. She didn't stop to realize that early on. Perhaps she was so overwhelmed with seeing him, and trying to make the night so perfect, she never stopped to look at the reality of what if. What if he is not the guy she believes him to be? Was this all a façade? Did he really mean what he said to her, about there being another chance? Or was he just looking to finish something they started over twenty years ago, and disappear on her for a second time?

"Jason? You're still up?" Charli asked in a soft gentle tone.

"Yea…Yea I'm still awake.   What's up?" Jason responded as he was half sleep.

"Nothing, never mind. Get some sleep." Charli responded with a disregarded answer.

Charli was hesitant to ask Jason, that come morning, if he will still be there with her. She made the decision not to. Again, it was her way of not ruining the moment. Her night was as perfect as she could have ever imagined it to be. So, she decided to sleep on it, as she slept in Jason's arms, and thenight was ended with a kiss to her frontal lobe and one final kiss on her lips.

"Actually, do you think we could go at it one more time?" Charli asking Jason in the now dark bedroom.

Jason responded with sincerity, "Charli, I'm forty-two years old, and I gave you three rounds. Like, relax. That's allyou're getting from me tonight."

The break of dawn arrived, Charli is still in bed, but Jason is absent from the picture. Charli begins to make slow motion gestures in the bed. She awakens herself by feeling the empty space on the mattress. She opened her eyes and saw no sign of Jason; she was unbelievably devastated. It was déjà vu; it felt like she turned the other cheek, and he slapped her harder than the first time he walked out on her. She didn't even bother to get out of bed, she just broke down into her reserved tears, completely wrapped up in her bed sheets.

But as she continued to ball her eyes out, she began to smell something coming from her kitchen. She immediately got out of bed, put on a tank top, her panties and her bathrobe, and looked down the staircase. She didn't know who was down there, being that Jason's clothes were removed from thestairs, from last night.

"Hello!" She shouted but didn't get an answer.

She then went to her nightstand dresser, grabbed her pepper spray, and went down the stairs; only to find her one true love, standing there in his black Armani boxers, with a pan in his hand, filled with scrambled eggs.

"Good morning, I figured this time, instead of deviled eggs, we have some scrambled eggs." Jason said as he remembered Charli was eating a deviled egg, when she openedthe door, and they met for the first time.

Charli dropped the pepper spray on the floor, covered her mouth as she began to shed more tears. Jason put the pan back on the stove and went over to comfort Charli. Charli hugged Jason with such tightness, as she didn't want to let him go.

"Hey, hey. What's going on? What's wrong?" Jason asked Charli.

Charli responded as she tried to control her sniffling, "I...Ijust thought that when I woke up, that you weren't going tobe here. I thought you were going to disappear on me again."

Jason had no choice but to understand where Charli was coming from. He understood why she would feel that way but assured her that was not going to happen for a second time.

As Jason wiped Charli's tears away, he said to her, "Everything that I always wanted in a woman, is in you. Leaving you the first time, I had my reasons, but shitty reasons to say the least. But as of today, you and I, I believe we are truly meant to be together now. Just you and me. And I will never, ever leave you again. You are the true love of my life. If we can make this work, if we can be together, you would make me the happiest man in this thing we call life. Let us put all the past behind us now and share this one life together."

"I would really love that. Okay, just you and me." Charli said as she looked up at Jason's face, gave him a kiss, and smiled with satisfaction.

Afterwards, Charli and Jason sat down at the kitchen table and had a very calm and casual conversation over breakfast. Just two people in love, enjoying each other's company. As they were eating scrambled eggs, along with avocado and toast, Charli briefly excused herself from the kitchen table, and went up the stairs into her bedroom closet. In her closet, she had this vintage style chest, filled with some of her old modeling photos, magazines and ads she was featured in. But what she also kept in the chest, was something very special. Something very near and dear to her heart. Can you guess what it is? It was Jason's Pink Floyd t-shirt. If you remembered, Jason left without a shirt on, he left his Pink Floyd shirt on the chair by the swimming pool. That was the only thing Charli had left of Jason, so she kept his Pink Floyd shirt all this time. As she took the shirt out of the chest, she slowly brought it to her face, and began to smell it. The shirt still had the scent of the Old Spice fragrance as she smelled the shirt, cruising back into memory lane. It put such a smile on her face. She then brought the shirt with her down the stairs, hiding it behind her back, with the intention of surprising Jason.

"I have something to show you," Charli said with a smirk on her face.

Jason responded with sarcastic humor, "Oh God, I hope it's not an ice pick and then you'll to stab me to death likeBasic Instinct?

As Charli rolled her eyes and gave off some giggles, she showed Jason what she was hiding behind her. Charli opened up the shirt and held it with her fingertips, as if it was a banner. At first, for a split second, Jason observed the shirt, but didn't put two and two together right away. Then when he realized that it was his Pink Floyd shirt that he left at the pool that fourth of July night, he was rather dumbfounded, as well as feeling a bit guilty.

"Wow, I can't believe you still have this." Jason said as Charli handed him the shirt.

"It was the only thing left of you that I had to remember." Charli said as she just stood there looking at him.

As Jason looked at Charli, he then looked at the shirt, and looked back at Charli and said, "I'm so sorry Charli. I know I broke your heart. But I'm willing to make that up to you. As long as it takes."

Since it was Sunday morning, and they both were off for the day, Charli asked Jason if he would like to take a walk over by the Central Park Lake. He was okay with that. Him and Hash

Brown got along quite well. Hash Brown was licking Jason's face like there was no tomorrow. As they both were getting ready for their afternoon outing, Charli received a call from Mary, David's wife.

"Hi my dear, how are you doing today?" Mary asked Charli.

"Hey Mary, I'm doing great actually, just about to head out in a bit. What's up?" Charli responded as she put on her black jeans and burgundy knee-high boots.

As Charli and Mary began to talk, Charli told Mary about her evening with Jason. Charli asked Mary if she remembered Jason, and without hesitation, Mary said, "of course I remember Jason. I also remembered how you drooled over him."

Charli had to get something off of her chest to Mary. Charli looked down the staircase to make sure Jason wasn't listening, she went into her bathroom and told this to Mary, "You know, I really do not have a clue where I would have ended up, if you and David didn't bring me into your home and accepted me as your family. Honestly, I would have probably taken my own life, years ago, had it not been for your love and support for all those years. All those years of therapy, being that you are a therapist, you got me through a lot. I just want you to know, even though you never had a daughter, you have always been like a mother to me. No, you are my mother, you are the only mother I've ever known, and you are the best mother any daughter could ever ask for. I love you, David, and Matthew so much. "

A brief moment of silence occurred. All Charli could hear on the other line was Mary's sniffling and a broken voice. "You have no idea how much that means to me Charli, and I love you too, very, very much."

As Charli said goodbye, she walked out of the bathroom and sat on the side of her bed for a moment, with theedge of her phone pressed against her chin. What she said to Mary was well overdue, and she was just so relieved and happyto finally say what she said.

"Hey Charli, are you ready to head out?" Jason asked at the bottom of the stairs.

"Yes, I'm coming down now." Charli responded.

Eleven minutes goes by, a perfect picture is what you see. You see Charli, Jason, and Hash Brown taking a nice brisk walk around the Central Park Lake, on a beautiful angelic day. As they walked, they exchanged a few words here and there. Hash Brown, sniffing away at the autumn leaves and cracked eggcorns as Jason was holding the leash. As Charli looked at the two of them, she turned around and looked over at the Central Park Lake. As she looked, she began to reflect. She thought about her life; she acknowledged where she made her mistakes, and where she could have done things better. But for the very first time in her life, she can look at her life with no regrets.

As she looked over to the park bench, she saw a woman sitting by herself, reading the same book that she read by Camella Deltona called, "*You're Too Alive.*" One may say that is pure coincidence, but Charli clearly knew, that was nothing but pure fate. Charli learned that having faith in fate would allow her to overcome any obstacle that life would ever throw at her. She learned that even after all she's been through, she does not have to live the rest of her life being a victim to anyone or anything. Charli has now, more than ever, become a true believer. A true believer in love, in her faith, and most importantly, a believer in second chances. This was Charli's chance.

She Taught Her Daughter (09/5/20 11:50 p.m.)

Sixteen years old, under the roof of her mother's,
A fatherless daughter, no sisters or brothers.
Workaholic mom, arrives home late at night,
Daughter doesn't like it, daughter and mom had a fight.
Daughter said, "I barely know who you are, you're a stranger to me,"
Mother said, "I work so hard, once you raise kids without a man, you'll see."
Daughter said, "it's not my fault another woman took dad away,"
Her mom said, "I don't deserve that, but for the record, I'm glad he's away."
Stressed out mom, clueless daughter,
Mom pours a glass of clear liquid, but it's not water.
She pours another and another, how many will she drink?
The daughter can be a little heartless to her mom, she doesn't stop to think.
The daughter says, "mom I'm sorry, I didn't mean to upset you,"
Mother responded, "it's okay baby; even I have regrets too."
She hugs her mother, but her mother had something to say,
After her mother told her, she respected her at the end of the day.
Her mother said, "to keep a long story short,
Before you were born, your father begged me to abort."
Her father was beating her mother,
All the overnights; always cheating, one after the other.
So she said, "I'm keeping this baby, I'll take care of her myself,"
She went through hell carrying her, pregnancy took a toll on her health.
Her water breaks, the time has come,
Excited about what she'll have, a daughter or a son.
Squeezing and pushing, ready to bring life into this world,
She hears a cry, it's a beautiful baby girl.

She raises her daughter, practically on her own,
Excessive arguments with her baby's father on the phone,
His deadbeat philosophy was set in stone.
Mother says, "we're better off without him, but I have to work,"
Daughter responded, "I didn't know mom, and you're right, we're better off, he's a jerk.
She begs her daughter to never let a man tear her apart,
She said, "stand on your own two feet, stay strong, and follow your heart."

The Forbidden Lake   (12/25/20 12:12 p.m.)

An afternoon ride down a woody, everlasting Pennsylvania road. Summer is almost gone, as this group of teenagers are looking to get the most out of the very last days of summer vacation, before they head off to college. Well, at least three out of the six are soon to be college students, and equipped with a full ride. Patricia was accepted to Princeton University on a full academic scholarship, Cameron is headingto Vanderbilt University on a football scholarship, and as for Tiffany, the wealthy one, her parents have fully paid for all four years in advance. As for the others, Stokely, JoJo, and William, their future plans are rather undecided.

she is nothing more but a spoiled, whinny, rich, "always gets her way" whore.And they would be absolutely correct, she is all of the above. However, she does have certain qualities to her. She is a generous person, she always gives Jo Jo and Patricia her high- end clothes that she never wore, with the price tags still hanging off the clothes. As a matter of fact, it was Tiffany's idea to invite all of her friends to this empty cabin for a weekend getaway before summer ends. Fully paid for at her expense, well, her parents' expense, that she "borrowed."

With Tiffany's allowance, she hired a limousine driver to take her and the others up to the cabin. A superficial, bright orange Hummer limousine, as well as an all-black Denali Yukon, to carry everyone's luggage. As the six of them are overly excited for this trip, having a ball in the limo, drinking champagne and blasting music from their favorite artists such as Drake, Young Thug, and Travis Scott. Tiffany, already popping another bottle, the group begin to socialize about what to expect at this soon to be occupied cabin.

"Hey yo, Tiff, what did your parents tell you about this cabin?" Cameron projected over the loud music.

"Well, I did my own research when I booked the cabin online. It was occupied by some people a couple of years ago but has never been used since. I thought it'd be super dope for a weekend trip." Tiffany responded as she turned the music down a few notches.

"Did anyone bother to bring…Miss Jackson?" William asked the other five.

A brief moment of silence as William looked at the other five in the limo. If you are wonder what William is referring to when he asked about "Miss Jackson," give it a few minutes, and you will definitely know exactly what he is talking about.

"I take that as a no?" William said as no one responded to him.

"I think I have some in my pink Birkin bag." Tiffany said to William.

As they were only five minutes away from their destination, according to the limo driver's GPS, there was a startling huge pop. A pop that had the whole Hummer limo swerving on the road, as one of the tires blew out from underneath. The driver on the Denali Yukon slammed on his breaks, as the Hummer continued to swerve on the road.Barely missing the incoming traffic, all six are in the back of the limo, terrified; Tiffany, JoJo, and Patricia are screaming atthe top of their lungs; praying for Jesus to grab the wheel. Finally, the limo driver managed to gain control of the steering, slammed on the breaks and came to a full stop as the front of the limo unfortunately kissed an enormous oak tree. Falling fragments of bark began to land on the hood and roof of the Hummer limousine. The limo was totaled.

"Is everyone okay?" Stokely asked, as they all impacted horribly in the back of the limo.

"Yea, yea I'm okay." William slowly responded.

Miraculously, none of them in the back of the limo were seriously injured. A few bruised marks on JoJo's arm, William suffered a sore shoulder, as he landed on the bar side of the limo, knocking over some empty champagne bottles. But everyone else were okay, aside from being shocked of the sudden impact. As they all got out of the back seat of the limo, they looked around, and saw nothing but the surroundings of oak trees, out in the middle of nowhere, with a few birds chirping here and there. The driver in the Denali Yukon slowly pulled over behind the wrecked Hummer. As he got out of the truck, he ran over to check on the six frightened teenagers.

"Are you guys alright?" The Yukon driver asked as he ran over to comfort them.

"Yes Rico, I think so." Tiffany responded.

The teenagers began to grow worried, as the driver of the Hummer did not exit out of the driver's seat. They were afraid that he was seriously injured, or even worse, that he was dead. Cameron then began to slowly walk over to the driver's seat. As he approached the driver's seat, he let out a heavy scream.

"Ooohhhhh, FUCK!" Cameron screamed as he saw the dead limo driver and turned his back away from the traumatizing scene.

"Oh my God, Cam, what is it?" Tiffany asked as she breathes heavily, terrified at what she is about to see.

As Tiffany and the others walk towards the driver's seat, they see the driver's bloody head, smashed through the windshield, with one eye missing. Tiffany, Patricia, and JoJo gave the most frightening ensemble of a scream they could ever possibly give. Even the birds were startled, flying out from the trees. It was the most graphic scene any of these teenagers ever laid eyes on. Rico, the Yukon driver, walked over to the driver's seat to have a look.

"Jesus, I have to call someone, right now." Rico said as he pulled out his phone.

As Rico makes the call, he begins to walk away from the scene and the others. Talking on his phone rather very professionally, calmly, and collectively. Being that this is not the first time Rico has ever saw someone's corpse, it didn't scare him to look at the body and make close observations. Rico, who is a large, six-foot-four-inch, Columbian man, who served in the U.S. military for fifteen years, and is now the personal bodyguard for Tiffany and her family. He's seen it all, enough bloodshed to fill Niagara Falls, enough corpses to make you want to leave the military, as he did, suffering from post-traumatic stress disorder.

"Guys just stay back, wait by the Yukon while I talk to the dispatcher." Rico said to the group.

Walking back to the Yukon, Stokely spotted something on the side of the road, something rather unusual. As he got close, the shiny object begins to appear much clearer. It was a broken arrow. The broken arrow was also next to the debris of the blown-out tire. After seeing the remains of the tire and the broken arrow, Stokely begins to speculate that this was no accident, but rather someone is out there, watching them right now.

"Yo, you guys have to see this shit, like right now." Stokely said, calling over the rest of the group to show them what he found.

"What are we looking at Stoke?" William asked with his eyebrows raised up in confusion.

Stokely responded as he picked up the broken arrow, "Look, someone shot this arrow into the tire, this wasn't an accident."

As all of them gathered around in a circular-like position, observing the broken arrow, they began to observe the woody environment that surrounded them. Not knowing who else could be out there, this situation certainly ingested a course of fear into all of them.

"Rico, you need to see this!" Tiffany said to Rico as he was still on the phone.

Rico lifted up his index finger, as he was giving the gesture of saying, "I'll be there in one minute." Tiffany then decided to call her mother. As she was dialing the number, she quickly hung up, as she forgot that her parents were away, on their own weekend getaway in Bermuda.

"Fuck my life, I forgot they went away too." Tiffany said to the rest of the group.

"Stoke, let me see that arrow." Patricia asked Stokely

Patricia was very curious towards the broken arrow. She studied things such as artifacts and ancient findings. In fact, she plans to study Archaeology when she goes to Princeton University. As Patricia examines the broken arrow, she immediately noticed something on the arrow that she recognized from an old book she read several times. The broken arrow had symbols and words engraved in the arrowhead, as well as the shaft. Patricia, being as intelligent and witty as she is, she begins to translate what was engraved on the broken arrow.

"We, we will have our re…That's all I can get from this part of the arrow. We have to find the other part." Patricia said as she examined the broken arrow.

"We will have our *re*? What the fuck is *re*?" Cameron said with aggressive concern.

"JUST LOOK FOR THE FUCKING OTHER HALF JIZZ FACE!" Tiffany shouted at Cameron.

"Hey, don't fucking scream at me, we don't need to look for some Goddamn arrow, we need to get the fuck outta here. Trip is cancelled." Cameron said, firing back at Tiffany.

As Rico made his way back over to the group, he said to them, "Okay, okay, okay, listen. Let's all calm down, take a breather. I just got off of the phone with the dispatcher. Some good news and some bad news. The bad news is we are out in the middle of fucking oblivion. It's going to take at the very least an hour or so before police or paramedics get here. But the good news is we are just a few minutes away from the cabin. So, we can all just pile up in the Yukon, drive over to the cabin, and wait for them there."

They all looked at each other, with no other alternatives in mind, and agreed that was the better decision to make. But Patricia was very adamant about finding the second half of the arrow. As the others made their way to the Yukon, Patricia began to look around for the other half.

"Patricia, come on, we have to go." William said to her.

"We have to find that other half," Patricia said as she looked, stepping on the twigs and dead leaves, creating the sounds of nature.

"Miss, we have to get going, please." Rico said to Patricia.

Patricia then stood there, holding the broken arrow. As she took one last look before heading into the Yukon with the others, she had no luck, finally gave up, and headed to the truck. Patricia realized, looking for the second half of the broken arrow in all of these leaves, would be like looking for a teardrop in a lake. Speaking of lakes, that is exactly what is next to the cabin that they are heading to.

As they arrived at the cabin, they got out of the truck and took a look around. Even after the traumatic event these teenagers had just endured, they could not help but embrace the beauty of such a place. The view was absolutely astonishing. A beautiful lake, reflecting every tree that surrounds it. As for the cabin, it was like a mansion made of wood. A cozy lookingtwo-story cabin, shaped like the letter "L." The whole scenery looked like something out of a Bob Ross painting; a very quiet, isolated environment.

"Okay, well, I have the keys to the cabin. I kind of want to change out of this outfit and burn it now." Tiffany said as she grabbed her pink Birkin bag.

"Did any of you guys bring food?" JoJo asked the ensemble.

"Well, I brought snacks, soup, and shit. Tiff said we could go finishing at the lake, but I guess not anymore." Cameron saidas he heads toward the cabin, following behind Tiffany.

"Rico, can you grab the rest of my stuff and bring it in please?" Tiffany asked Rico.

"Of course, Ms. Martins. Right away." Rico responded, as he only addresses Tiffany as Ms. Martins.

As the rest of them grabbed their belongings, JoJo stayed behind by the Yukon. She made a call to her father, to make him aware of the situation. But when she called, she did not receive an answer. So, her plan B was to give her mother a call, but unfortunately, she hasn't talked with her mother in over a year. JoJo and her mother were not exactly the best of friends. Her mother is a functioning alcoholic, who continuously denies her disease. It came to the point where JoJo couldn't stand the sight of her mother. So, JoJo thought it was best to distance herself from her mother, until she got herself together. But after well over a year, not much has changed. JoJo then decided to call her father again and then left a voice message:

"Hey poppa bear, um, I don't even know where to begin. Well for starters, we made it to the cabin. But unfortunately, we didn't make it all in one piece. We had an accident, but I am okay, my friends are okay, and we are just waiting for the police and paramedics to arrive at the cabin. The limo driver, he's not doing so good, so we asked them to bring paramedics. I don't entirely know where the hell we are, but I'll let you know as soon as possible. Again, I'm okay."

In the meantime, JoJo took a few panoramic shots of the beautiful five o'clock view and made her way into the cabin. As she walked in, everyone was sitting around, with not much to say. William was laying across the couch, sipping on a warm can of beer, Stokely was pacing back and forth in the kitchen, eating a bag of Potato Chips, Cameron was sitting down on the love couch, tossing his football in the air, as it spins, and Patricia was still pre-occupied with the broken arrow, deeply observing it. Tiffany took her bags up to the second-floor bedroom, as she went to shower and change her clothes. Rico went up to assist her.

"Have any of you guys bother to call your parents, to let them know what happened?" JoJo said as she held up her phone.

"Uh, yea, my parent doesn't give two shits, I'm not even wasting my time calling them." William said to JoJo.

"That's a definite no for me JoJo, as we all know." Stokely said with a melancholy look his face.

"Oh Stoke, I'm so sorry to even bother to ask that." JoJo said with remorse.

Stokely has unfortunately been dealing with grief and trauma prior to what has recently occurred. One night, Stokely's parents were heading back home from their special anniversary date. As they were driving, a drunk driver was flying at ninety-seven miles per hour, smacked dead into Stokely's parents' car, on the driver's side, killing his father instantly. Stokely's mother was still breathing, she made it to the hospital, but was pronounced dead shortly after. Of course, the drunk driver survived with minor scratches. But the judge threw the book at the drunk driver for double manslaughter.

All of this tragically happened a month shy of Stokely's High School graduation.

"You know, what we just experienced today, I wouldn't have mind if I didn't make it. That way I could be with them. Stokely said as his eyes became filled with watery sorrow."

"Hey, Stoke, come on, let's go outside and suck up some of this fresh nature oxygen." Cameron said as he led Stokely out the cabin, with his hand on Stokely's shoulder.

As Patricia was sitting at the desk, she was unable to reach a signal on her phone. It seems that JoJo was the only one who had a signal, or who cared to call her parents. But Patricia wanted to get to the bottom of the broken arrow, so she asked JoJo if she could use her phone, to do more research on the symbols of the broken arrow. As Patricia looked up the arrow on Google with JoJo's phone, she began to compare the symbols that were engraved on the broken arrow, to the symbols that were showed in the Google images. What she found was absolutely gruesome.

As Patricia researched what she could about the broken arrow, she said this to JoJo and William, "According to these articles and the book I read, this arrow belongs to the lost tribe of Redwater. Redwater was among the very first Native

Americans, they actually lived in this very same environment we are at now. In the year 1441, the tribe of Redwater was invaded by this secret group of European settlers called "The Izan," (I-Zon), who were said to be the evilest living souls to ever walk the face of this earth. The Izan came to the tribe of Redwater's land, and said they would like to live amongst them, but Redwater would have to surrender their rules and traditions, as well as surrender the majority of their land for the people of the Izan.

With the challenge of understanding and communicating with each other, due to each group speaking a different language, the tribe of Redwater refused such a nonsensical offer and asked The Izan to leave their land and go back to their own. But the Izan were far from taking any rejections. One night, while the tribe of Redwater were sleeping, the Izan came and brutally slaughtered them in their sleep. It was an absolute, inhuman massacre, killing the men, women, even children and infants. The Izan would take pregnant women, slice open their pregnant wombs with dull knives, to make the pain more crucifying. They did that right in front of the men and set the women on fire. Afterwards, one by one, the Izan slid the throats of the men. In that one night, the Izan killed over three hundred natives of the Redwater tribe. Legend has it, that all the bodies the Izan killed, they tossed them in that verysame lake, right out there. There was so much blood in the lake from all the bodies, that the lake turned completely red. That is how the tribe later on received their name, Redwater.

In their tribe, the was a shaman; he was among the last who were killed. Translated from their native language, these were the shaman's dying words before the Izan killed him, "Oblivion, oblivion, I bequeathed to you the echo ofmy last breath. Take me into your home of enchanted mystery. Take me to the unknown. Curses on this land and on this lake. Those who awake us at rest, shall join us."

Legend also has it, that to this day, there are still some Redwater tribesmen living amongst these very woods, who does not want anyone here, disturbing their ancestors who are at rest. That is why it is called the Forbidden Lake."

"Damn, so what you're saying is that the natives from this lost tribe are the ones who shot the arrow into the tire?" William asked Patricia with a startled look on his face.

"I, I don't know who could have done it, but I'm sure whoever is out there, they definitely don't want us here." Patricia responded.

"Well, I think once the police get here, we should just pack our shit and get the hell out of here." JoJo said anxiously.

As Patricia, William, and JoJo continue to conversate about what they just learned, in comes Cameron and Stokely. Stokely didn't say a word, just went straight to the restroom.

"How's he doing?" JoJo asked Cameron.

"Eh, he'll be alright, Cameron responded mildly.

"Hello, my people, and how are we doing so far?" Tiffany said, as she finally came down, freshly showered with her new White folded button up shirt and denim shorts outfit.

"Hey Tiff, we need to like, you know, eighty-six this whole weekend getaway. I'm not feeling it anymore. I meancome on, the limo driver is out there, dead with his head clean through the windshield." William said with urgency.

Tiffany responded, "Okay, I agree, but we can't just leave without getting everything situated with the cops. Rico said they will be coming through pretty soon, right Rico?"

"Right Ms. Martins. In fact, I'm going to drive back out there right now, and wait for the police to arrive." Rico said as he grabbed the keys to the Yukon and headed out the door.

Before Rico walked out, he gave everyone the ground rules and told them to not leave the cabin, under any circumstances, no exceptions. Patricia then showed Rico the broken arrow, told him what it means, and begged him to look for the other half while he waited for the police; Rico agreed.

As he left, the five of them began to discuss what Patricia researched about the lost tribe of Redwater, and how the broken arrow ties to what has happened.

"I call absolute BULLSHIT!" Cameron shouted as he was told the story of the Redwater tribe.

"Yea, I mean, I'm sorry, but I'm going to have to agree with Cameron. I mean who's to say that the limo driver simply ran over the broken arrow on the road, and that's how it blew out the tire. I bet you that's how it happened." Tiffany saidas she fixed herself a drink in the kitchen.

"No, someone definitely had to of shot the arrow from a distance. Those tires are too thick to have them just blow out by running over the arrow." Patricia responded.

As the Sun begins to take it's leave for the day, Rico headed back to the limousine crash site. He parked right behind the limo, the same spot where he parked when the limo crashed. Being that Rico is a trained veteran, he took no chances and brought his fully loaded, Glock 45 9mm. Rico began to walk towards the limo, much more alert than what he was earlier. As he came closer to the driver's seat, he was expecting to still see the limo driver, dead with his head through the windshield. But what Rico saw, put him in a much more alerting and panicking situation; an unexpected scene.

The limo driver's body was gone. Rico opened the car door, looked at both seats, and then began to look around the whole limousine. There was absolutely no sign of him. Until Rico caught wind of something, several feet away from the limo, in a pile of leaves. There was more debris from the blown-out tire of the Hummer limo. In the pile of leaves and debris, Rico saw a shiny looking stick, somewhat similar to what the broken arrow looks like. As Rico came close to the shiny stick, he picked it up, and what he saw, he knew right away that he was not alone. The shiny stick was the other half of the broken arrow. But stuck on the broken part, was the eyeball of the limo driver. Rico's own eyes popped out of his head, in absolute shock at what he's seeing right now. The tiny hairs on the back of his neck were all standing stiff as a board. He damn near turned into a porcupine. Rico immediately pulled out his Glock 45, and gave himself a panoramic view of his surroundings. As he took the other half of the broken arrow with him, he removed the eye, and made his way back to the Yukon, slammed and locked the door.

As he starts the truck, he sits there as darkness bleeds into the sky to make the night. The only lights he had access to, were the lights from the truck. As he looks at his phone to call and warn Tiffany, he begins to hear something, he hears drums. Not the kind of drums you would go crazy for at a rock concert. But the kind of drums that lets you know, your life is in danger. Rico's heart was racing so fast. The pace of his heart was even in sync with the pace of the drums.

Rico then decided to call the police again. He dialed "911," and put the phone to his head. As he looked up at his rearview mirror, he dropped his phone between his lap, and screamed as if he saw the devil himself. What he saw, would make your worst nightmare look like a fairy tale. What he saw, will make you turn on all the lights in your house, right now.

"JESUS CHRIST! WHAT THE FUCK IS THAT?" Rico screamed as he pulled off, heading back to the cabin.

Back at the cabin, the whole group began to pack their bags, as their enthusiasm for this weekend getaway came to a drastic end. Cameron growing a little paranoid, he asked Tiffany if she had "Miss Jackson," somewhere in her bag.

"Here, I thought I had her, but all I could find were my cigarettes." Tiffany said as she handed Cameron a couple of loosies.

"I'm not really a fan of cigarettes, but I guess that will have to do." Cameron said as he was heading out the cabin to smoke.

"Hey, where do you think you're going? You know Rico told us to stay inside until he came back." JoJo said to Cameron.

"Yo relax, I'm just going out to take a few puffs and that's it. Unless you guys want me to smoke in here, I can do that too?" Cameron said as he grown irritated.

As Cameron walked out of the cabin onto the front porch, he made his way down the wooden stairs, towards the dock by the lake. The water was dark and still, no reflection of the trees, as everything was pitch black; except for the lights shinning on the trees near the cabin. As Cameron stood there on the dock, he pulled out his lighter, covering the flame to ignite the cigarette. He lifted his head up as he blew out the smoke of intoxicating nicotine. As he took another puff, he began to hear something. The sounds that Cameron was hearing, were the same familiar drums that Rico heard out at the crash site. The sound of the drums was beginning to grow louder as it came closer to Cameron. As if the sound had heavy footsteps. Cameron begins to feel a tingling sensation on the back of his neck, as if someone was creeping up behind him. Too afraid to turn around, his body begins to quiver, and quiver, and quiver, until he quickly whipped his upper body around, and saw absolutely no one. The sound of the drums went silent, hearing nothing but the water of the lake, soaking up the wood of the dock. As Cameron slowly turned his body around, now facing the lake, he couldn't help but laugh at himself, as he realized that all of this Redwater and broken arrow talk has made him paranoid.

He took one final drag out of his cigarette, blew out the smoke, and then flicked his lit cigarette into the lake. As he was walking back to the cabin, something unexplainable happened.

"Ouch, son of a BITCH!" Cameron projected as he was hit by something hot on the side of his face.

Cameron quickly turned around, facing the lake again as he placed his hand of the left side of his face, the side that was hit by a hot object. As he looked, he saw nothing, he heard nothing, until he looked down at the dock platform, and saw something he couldn't possibly believe. He saw the cigarette that he flicked into the lake. He picked it up and saw that the cigarette was still lit, and smoke rising out of it. Mind you, the cigarette was completely dry.

As Cameron held up the cigarette and looked out at the lake, he knew at that very moment that the whole Redwater tale had some truth to it. Cameron slowly back pedaled his way off of the dock, making his way back to the cabin. As he makes his way back, he was blinded by the lights of Rico's truck, as Rico made it back from the crash site.

"What the hell are you doing out here? I told you guys to stay inside." Rico said angerly as he pulled Cameron's arm and directed him into the cabin.

"Yo Rico man, there's some supernatural shit going on out here. I think we should just leave right now, and let the police find the limo driver on their own." Cameron said as he walks back into the cabin with Rico.

"Well, somebody, or something actually beat the police to it. The limo driver's body wasn't there when I pulled up." Rico said as he took a deep breath.

"What the hell do you mean he wasn't there Rico?" Tiffany asked with a terrified look in her eyes.

"He wasn't there Ms. Martins. I went to the crash site, and when I looked at the driver's seat, his body was gone, and..." Rico responded as he hesitated to finish what else he saw.

"And what Rico?" Patricia asked as they all moved towards Rico.

As Rico looked at all five of their frightened faces, he realized he couldn't hide the fear on his own face. Rico then told them this, "I, I saw something out there. I don't know who or what the hell it was. I never saw something like it in my life, nor do I want to see it ever again. So, if you guys do not mind, I would appreciate it if you all get your shit together, put it in the truck, and we get the fuck outta here."

Tiffany asked, "But wait, what about the cops Ric…"

"There ARE NO COPS COMING, MS. MARTINS!" Rico shouted at Tiffany with a frustrated tone.

"What do you mean there are no cops coming?" JoJo asked Rico.

"When I tried to call the cops the first time, when the limo crashed, I couldn't get a signal. I tried calling them multiple times. You guys were already so scared, I just had to tell you something so that you wouldn't panic. So, I lied about the cops being on their way." Rico said with such a guilty look on his face.

"Oh, you fuc…Oh, that's great, that was a BRILLANT idea. Way to go Rico, you're definitely going to get the medal of honor for this. Cameron sarcastically said to Rico.

Rico then took Cameron's five-foot, ten-inch frame, thrown him up against the wall, looked in Cameron's eyes and said this, "You better shut the fuck up, right now. There is something out there, and if any of you want to make it out of this nightmare alive, you better do EXACTLY what I say, when I say it!"

As Rico had Cameron pinned up against the wall, the second half of the broken arrow was sticking out of Rico's leg pocket. Patricia saw the shiny stick and noticed it immediately.

"Oh my God, you found it! You found the second half of the arrow." Patricia said enthusiastically.

"GET THE FUCK OFF ME, MAN!" Cameron said pushing Rico off of him.

Rico then pulled out the second half of the broken arrow and handed it to Patricia. Patricia then went to the desk to grab the first half of the broken arrow. As she put two and two together, she discovered the full description that was engraved. As she translated the meaning, she turned around to look at everyone else as her face dropped.

"What does it say Patricia?" William asked.

"We will have our revenge." Patricia said as she walked over to the window facing the lake.

As the room went into complete silence, they all looked at each other with the same idea in their minds. It was at that very moment, they knew they were not welcomed in that cabin, or near the lake. It was time for them to go. As they finished packing, they all double checked to make sure they didn't leave anything behind, but unfortunately, they did; Stokely was missing. He never came out of the restroom when he walked in with Cameron. Cameron remembered that Stokely went straight to the bathroom, so he went to let Stokely know that everyone was packed and ready to go. At the end of the hallway, where the restroom is located, Cameron walked to it and repeatedly knocked on the door.

"Yo Stoke, come on man, we're getting out of here right now." Cameron said outside of the locked restroom door.

No answer: Cameron tried again with more intensity, but still there was no response. As everyone's patience was growing thin, Rico then stepped in and gave it a try.

"Get your ass out of the bathroom, right now! We're leaving. Don't make me kick the door open." Rico said, pounding his massive fist onto the restroom door.

But still, no answer. Rico was left no choice but to use his size fourteen foot and kick the door wide open. Splinters and woodchip fragments went everywhere. But shockingly, Stokely was nowhere in sight. As Rico and Cameron walked into the bathroom, they saw nothing but the remains of the broken door on the floor, with an open window, and a gust of wind blowing through the curtains. Stokely went a-wall.

"Stoke, Stoke!" Cameron shouted as he poked his head out of the open bathroom window.

"Come on, let's go." Rico said as he grabbed the rest of Tiffany's bags and walked out of the cabin.

"Woah, we are not leaving here without Stokely." Cameron said as he followed Rico out of the cabin.

"WE DON'T HAVE TIME TO FUCKING PLAY HIDE AND GO SEEK! Your friend wants to take off and go on his own, good luck to him." Rico said to Cameron as the rest of the ensemble watched near the Yukon truck.

"Wait, Stokely's gone? Gone where?" JoJo asked.

"I don't know, but we have to find him. We can't leave here without him." Cameron said with much concern.

"Rico, *please*. Just give it ten minutes. Maybe he'll show up then." Tiffany said to Rico as she begged him to wait.

"Ms. Martins, your parents asked me to look after YOU, they didn't hire me to look after your friends, who just run off into the woods, surrounded by God knows who or whatthe hell is out there." Rico said to Tiffany.

"Please Rico, please. I'm not asking you to playRambo. Just ten minutes; ten minutes and then we'll go, okay?" Tiffany said as she pleaded with Rico.

As Rico took a look at his watch, he confirmed that he'll delay their departure. Even though their bags werepacked and ready to go, they all decided to wait back in the cabin. Cameron knew that Stokely would not be back within those ten minutes, and he also knew that Rico was definitely going to leave as soon as those ten minutes were up. So, Cameron stepped up and showed some sign of bravery.

"Okay listen you guys, why don't I just go and look for Stokely? He can't be but so far from here. Cameron said to the rest of them.

"I don't know Cam, that seems too risky right now. Why don't we just wait here? Maybe he just had to walk it off." William said to Cameron.

"Wait a minute, did he have his phone on him? JoJo, give him a call." Patricia said as she walked over to JoJo on the couch.

"That's a terrific idea Patricia, why didn't our dumb asses think of that before?" JoJo said as she dialed Stokely's number and put him on speaker.

The phone rang several times, but no answer fromStokely. The rest looked at each other with disappointment. As Rico gave the rest of the group a five-minute warning, he placed his Glock 45 and keys to the truck on the kitchen table, as he himself had to use the restroom. The clock was ticking, and Stokely was still out there, lost in the dark wilderness of the unknown.

"Guys, what are we going to do, Rico is serious, he's going to leave Stokely here. William said to the group.

"Oh, wait, this is Stokely calling back right now." JoJo said as she quickly answered her phone and put it on speaker.

"HEY, STOKE, WHERE ARE YOU? YOU HAVE TO COME BACK TO THE CABIN RIGHT NOW BUD!" Cameron shouted to Stokely through the speaker phone.

But the response they all heard, put more fear in their hearts than you can imagine. They did not hear Stokelytalking, they heard him screaming. Screaming at the top of hislungs, as if he was being tormented beyond human capabilities.

"HELLLLPPPPPP MEEEEE!" Stokely screamed through the phone.

"Hold on Stoke, I'm coming to save you. Don't hang up, keep talking to him!" Cameron said as he grabbed Rico's Glock 45 from the kitchen table and ran out of the cabin.

Rico hurried out of the restroom to see what all of the commotion was about. They told him that Stokely is in danger and Cameron went to find him. Rico then turned to the kitchen table, to only notice that his gun was missing.

"Please tell me, that fucking kid did not take my ONLY gun?" Rico said as he was absolutely appalled and livid.

Cameron ran off, faster than the speed of light. Using his track and football athleticism, as he leaped and hurdled over tree branches. Deeper and deeper he went into the woods. Completely surrounded by nothing but darkness and undeniable fear.

"STOKELY, STOKELY! WHERE ARE YOU?" Cameron shouted, causing eerie echoes.

He shouted Stokely's name some more, but not a sound bounced back, at least not the sound he wanted to hear. The sound Cameron heard, was the sound of laughter; creepy, demonic laughter. At that moment, Cameron did not know what to do. He didn't know whether he should stay to find Stokely, or leave, believing that he could possibly be next. The laughter continued, it was as if the laughter was a surround sound stereo, moving closer, louder.

"WHO, WHO IS THAT? WHO ARE YOU? ARE, ARE YOU REDWATER?" Cameron yelled as he held the gun up, shaking from head to toe.

After Cameron asked that question, the laughter stopped completely. He heard nothing, nothing but the heavy sounds of his breath. Then came along the sound of footsteps; one by one, as if they were coming towards him. Then came the sound of drums, the same eerie drums that he heard on the docks. With fear swimming through his body, Cameron had no other choice but to fire off a few shots, hoping to scare off whoever is out there. But the drums kept coming, closer and closer. He couldn't take it anymore, he decided to run back to the cabin. Faster and faster he ran, but the drums were able to keep up with him. Too afraid to look back, he stopped in his tracks and said this:

"Stokely, if you're there, show yourself right now."
Cameron said as the drums faded out.

Dead silence again, as Cameron held the gun with his finger on the trigger, he turned around and saw nothing but a pitch-black image of the unknown. In that moment, Cameron realized he still had his lighter in his pocket. He quickly pulled out his lighter, flicked that spark of light, with half of his terrified face now illuminated in the dark. Cameron heard nothing; he saw nothing. He then turned around and started to run back to the cabin. He stopped again, as he heard somethingcome behind him. As if something rolled and bounced off the ground like a large bumpy bowling ball. As Cameron turned around to see what that was, he bent down with his lighter, terrified to what he might find. He found it and immediately regretted it. What he found on the ground was Stokely, well, what was left of Stokely. Stokely was completely decapitated, his eyes were popped out of the sockets, and a bloody marking was carved on his forehead that said, "LEAVE." Cameron never ran as fast as he did out in those woods.

Back at the cabin, the rest of the group were losing it. They didn't know what to do, and Rico refused to leave without his gun. They had no other choice but to wait. But they didn't have to wait very much longer, as Cameron made his way backto the cabin.

"OPEN UP, OPEN THE FUCKING DOOR!"
Cameron said as he screamed, knocking on the front door.

"Jesus, Cameron what happened to you?" asked Tiffany Cameron.

But before Cameron could get a word out, Rico gave him a quick gut check. Cameron just fell to the floor, as he was already exhausted from running for his life.

"That was for taking my gun you son of a bitch!" Rico said as he pointed his gun at Cameron.

"Alright stop! Rico, please." Tiffany said as she tried to calm Rico down.

"Cameron, any luck with Stokely?" JoJo asked Cameron.

As Cameron looked up at everyone from the floor, he said with tears in his eyes, "He didn't make it." The five of them began to mourn in sorrow. Rico was rather adamant about getting the hell out of there as soon as possible. As they began to move, JoJo received a phone call. JoJo looked at her phone with a combination of confusion and terror, as it was Stokely calling her.

"You guys, look." JoJo said as she showed the rest of them who was calling.

"No fucking way, they have his phone." Cameron said as he saw Stokely's name on JoJo's phone.

"WELL ANSWER IT, GODDAMN IT!" Tiffany shouted at JoJo.

As JoJo answered her phone and put it on speaker, they couldn't believe whose voice they heard; it was Stokely's. Stokely's voice did not sound as normal, but rather possessed. As if this supernatural being is speaking through him. Through Stokely, this creepy, demonic entity came through and said:

"We warned you, but now it's too late. We will do to you, what the Izan did to *us*. Say your prayers, as we did not have our chance to pray."

That was enough to get them even more scared shitless. As they begin to head out, the cabin went completely black. The lights ceased to exist. Rico, trying to calm everyone down, and tell them to be as quiet as possible. They all remained in the cabin. Rico told William and Cameron to close and lock all the windows and back doors. Tiffany, JoJo and Patricia allwent to the kitchen to find the sharpest knives they could, to give themselves some form of protection.

"All the doors and windows are secured and locked." William said to Rico.

As the five of them came back together in the living room, Rico said this to them, "Listen to me very carefully. We have to get out of here, but what I'm going to do is… Shh, do guys here that?"

The eerie sound of footsteps was making its way on the wooden porch. They all remained silent, so quiet that you could hear an ant sneeze. The footsteps were walking all around the "L" shaped porch, but they did not see anyone out there. Could this be the spirits of the tribe of Redwater? The footsteps then began to fade out.

Rico, as quietly as he could, told the others that he was now going to head out to the Yukon truck first, and make sure the coast was clear.

"Once I get out to the truck, I want you three to come out first, then you two come out after." Rico said as he gives them an escape plan.

Rico walked over to the front door, as he opened it, he couldn't help but look down on the front porch. What he saw was something very startling. He saw a little moccasin, little as if it was made for a child. As he picked it up, it was soaking wet, as if it came directly from the lake. But as Rico looked down again, underneath the moccasin, there was a bloody print of the sole of the moccasin. Bloody footprints were all around the "L" shaped porch. Rico then dropped the moccasin on the ground, wiping off the blood from the palm of his hand, and had a change of plans. Once Rico saw that, he changed his plans and told all of them to run like hell to the Yukon truck. One by one they all went, as the truck was only twenty feet away from the cabin. Once they all made their way into the truck, shut and locked the doors, they had a sigh of relief. "Okay, we're out of here, let me just get my keys." Rico said as he reaches in his pocket to grab his keys.

As he didn't find his keys in one pocket, he searches for them in his other pockets. But his keys weren't on him. He then lifted his head up and began to have a cussing fit, as he realized that he left his keys on the kitchen table next to his gun, when he used the restroom.

"FUCK ME!" Rico said while they were all in the truck.

"I'll go get the keys." Cameron said.

"No, you stay in the truck. In fact, you all stay in the truck, is that clear?" Rico said as he prepared himself to walk back in the cabin.

Rico then opened the door to his truck, slamming the door with his left hand, and his right hand holding the gun. He begins to go into military mode, observing all of his surroundings, as if he was in Call of Duty. As the rest of the group watched Rico from the truck and made his way into the cabin, JoJo receives yet another call. Not a creepy call from Stokely's phone, but a call from her father. Remember earlierwhen she left her father a voice message? Well, he finally called her back. With such enthusiasm, she answered her phone and put her dad on speaker.

"Dad, oh my God, we need help! There's someone out here after us!" JoJo desperately said to her father.

"Okay, Okay, JoJo listen, I called the cops about thirty minutes ago. When you left that message, I had a gut feeling that things would just get worse, so I called them as soon as I heard the message. But they're on their way." JoJo's father said as the others listened in on the call.

"Okay dad, if I don't get to say this again, I love you."
JoJo said before she hung up.

BANG! BANG! BANG! That's all they heard, sitting in the truck. The cabin lit up with three blue flashes from the gun shots. As all five of them stared at the cabin from inside the truck, they began to see what they feared the most. They saw what appeared to be a little girl, coming out of the cabin. A native from the tribe of Redwater. All five of their eyes were dead focused on the little girl, scared to absolute death, as Rico is nowhere in sight. As they continue to watch, the little girl is still standing there, but then she was accompanied by a man, then came out a woman, and another, and another.

"Do not move an inch." Patricia said to the others.

"Where is Rico?" Tiffany softly said with fear throttling in her throat.

As soon as Tiffany said that, out came Rico. Rico, who was dressed in a black t-shirt, black cargo pants and tactical boots, came out of the cabin shirtless, with bloody cuts decorated all over his upper body. Rico was barely able to walk, but he made it halfway to the truck. As Rico tried to take another step, he dropped to one knee. Tiffany, who couldn't sit back and watch anymore, got out of the truck, and ran to Rico.

"Tiffany NO, get back in the truck!" Cameron screamed from inside the truck.

As Tiffany ran to Rico, she hugged the bloody aftermath of him. Being that Rico was her family's bodyguard for most of her life, she had a stronger bond with him that the others could not relate to. Her tears began to drop into his cuts and the wounds were far from ever being healed. With the final moments awaiting Rico, he said this to Tiffany:

"Its…It has been my honor to look after you and your family Ms. Martins. I made a deal with the Redwater tribe. I sacrifice my life, in return, they spare the rest of you guys. This is the way it has to be. Take the keys and never come back here."

"Rico, I can't leave you. Please…" Tiffany said as she uncontrollably cries her eyes out.

"You have to, leave right now, save yourself, and save the others. Leave, please leave now." Rico said as he is on his final leg.

Tiffany takes the keys, then gave Rico one last embrace of his wounded goodbye, looks at him as she back pedals to the truck, opens the door to the driver's seat, and starts the engine.

"Alright Tiff, we have what we need, lets drive off and get the hell out of here once and for all." Cameron said as he and the rest of them still looks out at Rico.

"TIFF, STEP ON IT NOW! William yelled as he tries to snap Tiffany out of it.

Tiffany then turns the stirring wheel to the left and drives off. As she drives, she can see Rico in the rearview mirror. As Rico sacrificed his life to save theirs, he stood tall on his two feet, looked to the night sky, and made his final statement: "Look ma, your boy's a hero."

As soon as he made peace with his sacrifice, three of those same shiny arrows went piercing through his already wounded body. One through his head, another through his stomach, and the last going through his heart. Tiffany saw his body drop in the rearview mirror, as they drove down the darkand woody road. One hand on the steering wheel, while the other was covering her mouth as she continued to cry.

Tiffany and the others continued to drive down the road, completely shocked about what they have just survived. Tiffany, driving down the dark road, tears overriding down her face. Cameron, who is sitting in the passenger seat, traumatized after what he encountered with Stokely. As for the rest of them, JoJo, Patricia, and William, they all played their parts, and survived. As they drove down the road, they saw a flickering of red and blue lights. Instantly aware that they were coming close to approaching the cops. As oneof the police officers flagged them down, Tiffany slowed down and came to a full stop beside the police officer. The officer noticed the blood stains on Tiffany's white shirt.

"Are you young folks alright?" The police officer asked, with his country accent.

"No, we barely escaped with our lives officer." Tiffany said as she begins to cry again.

"You guys went to Redwater didn't you?" The officer asked as if he already knew.

"You know about Redwater officer?" Cameron asked.

The officer responded, "Oh yes, that's been going on for centuries, with all the spirits and stuff. Then there's the cabin up there. The natives hide in the woods, shoot out your tires, then people stay up in the cabin. Usually there are no survivors, unless someone makes a sacrifice, which I'm assuming someone from your group did?"

"Yea, three sacrifices actually." William said to the officer.

"Well, consider yourselves the lucky ones; I hope none of y'all expected the police to show up, that's an automatic death sentence. We don't even have service for that area. And those heartless crooks always send people, such as yourselves, up there to the cabin, for a real nice expensive getaway, with no warnings. Goddamn realtors always take advantage of you rich kids. Same thing happened two years ago; group of kids like yourselves went to the cabin, it was about eight of them, come morning, only two were still alive. They came to us to tell us what happened. They said they saw the devil. A devil with drums. Well, y'all better get going now, stay on the path." The officer said as he stepped aside to let them go.

"Wait a minute officer. Do you know what the tribe of Redwater does with all the bodies?" Patricia asked.

The officer hesitated at first, and then said, "The tribe does the same thing to the bodies that the Izan did to them. They dump them into the lake, to keep the water red with people's blood. That's why they call it the forbidden lake; it's alive!"

As the officer walked back to his car, Tiffany then drives off, and doesn't look back. A weekend getaway turned into a night of unimaginable horror. With all that has happened, by the time Tiffany and the others return home, Tiffany will have an enormous amount of explaining to do. You see, Tiffany's parents knew very well about the forbidden lake, and made Tiffany swear to never step foot near that lake or cabin. But as I said in the very beginning, she is a spoiled, "always gets her way" whore, who lied and duped Rico and her friends into coming. And now, she has blood on her hands, forever.

<u>Conclusion</u>

Here we are, at the end of the road of this poetic journey. This was by far one of my most challenging pieces of literature I created so far. I took much risk with writing about certain topics. But I believe that is what being a writer is all about. Taking risks, reaching for boundaries that have never been reached before. I wanted to challenge myself and explore different thoughts and ideas.

As of right now, I feel that my poetic journey has reached its fullest potential, for right now. I am now taking my writing ventures to another direction. I believe it is time for me to step into the novel world. The two short stories that you read, "Charli's Chance" and "The Forbidden Lake," were precursors to my next book. I can't say just yet about what my next book will be. You will just have to wait and see when it is released. But what I will say is this, it will leave you dumbfounded. So, with all of that being said, I truly hope you have enjoyed this experience. I hope some of the imagery and profanity was not too graphic for you. I also hope that you continue to support my work and appreciate it. Because I appreciate you.

Thank You

First and foremost, I have to thank God for the blessing. Without God, none of this would have been possible. God most definitely guided me through, not just this book, but all four of them. Next I would like to thank you, the reader, for your time. I know poetry is not the easiest thing to read and understand. So, poetry readers always take a chance. I thank you all very much for the love and support. It means so much, and it is a very big deal for me.

I want to thank my mother and father for bringing me into this world. I thank, once again, my High School African American history teacher, Ms. Rich, for her spark of inspiration for me to start writing poetry. I thank my former college professor, Henry "Hank" Stewart again, for helping me with my writing craft. I also want to thank the few friends I have, and my family for all the love and support.

Lastly, I would like to thank those who are not even born yet. I thank you, the future readers, who will one day come across this book, read it, and it just may change your life. You may see your life through this poetry, and you may be inspired to become a writer, a poet. I thank you, the future readers, whether that is five, ten, twenty, or even a hundred years from now. I thank you guys in advance.

With all of that being said, I think we are finished with "*A Lonely Rose.*" I thank you all, I appreciate you, stay blessed, and until next time. Remember, you are too alive, enjoy your life to the very fullest. Plant your truest potential, watch it grow and blossom into greatness. Thanks again and take care. Also, I completely forgot about this poem, and decided to add this one at the very end of this book.

ABOUT THE AUTHOR

JORDAN WELLS was born and raised in East Orange, New Jersey. He graduated from Centenary University; earning a bachelor's degree in business, with concentrations in finance and marketing. He is also a professional actor, a member of the Screen Actors Guild-American Federation of Television and Radio Artists. His fourth book, "*A Lonely Rose*," is an addition to Wells' poetic collection. "*The Healing*," is Wells' third book. "*Mirrors and Reflections*" is Wells' sophomore book, his debut book, "*Logged Off: My Journey of Escaping the Social Media World*," was a monumental achievement in Wells' life, and will continue on with his creative writing ventures.

Made in the USA
Middletown, DE
21 April 2022